W9-BXZ-290

GHOSTS
OF THE
OLD WEST

By Earl Murray from Tom Doherty Associates

GHOSTS
OF THE
OLD WEST

EARL MURRAY

A TOM DOHERTY ASSOCIATES BOOK
NEW YORK

GHOSTS OF THE OLD WEST

This book is printed on acid-free paper.

A Tor Book
Published by Tom Doherty Associates, Inc.
175 Fifth Avenue
New York, NY 10010

Tor Books on the World Wide Web:
http://www.tor.com

Tor® is a registered trademark of Tom Doherty Associates, Inc.

Library of Congress Cataloging-in-Publication Data

Murray, Earl
    Ghosts of the old West / Earl Murray. — 1st Tor trade pbk. ed.
       p.   cm.
    "A Tom Doherty Associates book."
    Originally published: Chicago : Contemporary Books, c1988.
    ISBN 0-312-86795-6
    1. Ghosts—West (U.S.)   I. Title
BF1472.U6M87   1998
133.1'0978—dc21   98-20322
                                             CIP

First Tor trade paperback edition: October 1998

Printed in the United States of America

0 9 8 7 6 5 4 3 2 1

To my close friends: Mike and Sue,
Mouse and Magoo—
a great family, with tremendous spirit

Contents

Introduction

Paranormal occurrences have been with mankind throughout recorded time, and without question before. Especially
those regarding the dead. Visions or encounters of feeling or
sensation with what has commonly been termed ghosts or
spirits are widespread throughout the world. And because
ghosts are one of the more interesting and controversial forms
of psychic manifestation, reported sightings are still treated
with a great deal of skepticism—except by those who have experienced them.

The world of ghosts is no more visible in any other part
of the world than in the vast region of the western United
States. The Old West and the frontier of the last century have
spawned that which is unsettled. In this open and unsheltered
space tales of ghosts and the supernatural take every form.
They are widely associated with old houses and buildings of
various kinds—old hotels and theaters and mansions—as well

as old forts and battlegrounds, deserted stretches of highway, and other back-country locales.

The landscape itself, with vast panoramas of wilderness and open country—marked by dead trees and oddly formed cactus—can create illusions. But it is not illusion that makes an imprint on the mind of someone who has experienced a ghost. The unmistakable smell of chicken soup in California's Winchester House, when no soup of any kind was boiling, made a young caretaker aware that some presence existed besides her own. The sounds of whispering men and the swish of grass, as if someone were walking, convinced a college historian that there was another presence other than his own where he sat on a deserted Nebraska battlefield during one fall night.

What is it that produces a ghost? No one seems in absolute agreement. One theory is that the existence of happiness as well as stress in someone's earthly life manifests "benign" as well as "malevolent" ghosts. The possibility of violent death is often proposed as the reason for a certain ghost's presence. During the westward movement, the pioneers who came to unknown lands found themselves faced with incredible hardship and heartache. Soldiers and civilians alike did not survive long after reaching the western frontier. War and sickness, and often accidents or the elements, sent many to early graves.

But there are said to be hauntings by those who were so content with their earthly surroundings that they refuse to leave. Or is it some form of unfinished business? Arguments abound, like the one over the "Third Floor Ghost" inhabiting the guest lodge at Montana's famed Chico Hot Springs Resort. Known for its cuisine, relaxation, and frequent Hollywood guests, the resort also harbors this ghost, who it is said watches over the patrons and the caretakers. The story is remarkable, but inexplicable.

The western region was home to the supernatural long before the emigrant movement from the East and Midwest began. It is in the Old West that the Native Americans practiced their spiritual religion. Theirs was and, for those in touch with the old ways, still is a life based largely on reverence for the unexplained powers of the universe and the mind's abilities to use them. Their medicine is a sacred gift given to those who respect it. It is not to be abused. Bad medicine, as the term is loosely used, is no joke. There are qualities to American Indian medicine that go beyond the limits of life as we know it. That dimension is as boundless as the universe their medicine encompasses.

The work presented in this volume is intended to provoke thought with regard to the limitations of the human mind. Is it rational to believe in ghosts, or is it rational to scoff at those who do?

Ghosts have long been a part of folklore, always a topic during dark nights, whether in the city or deep in the woods. People who have never seen them talk about them in storybook fashion, bringing wide-eyed gasps and a few chuckles; those who have seen them are content to listen, usually guarding their experiences tightly while the others are entertained. They do not want anyone laughing at them, for their experience is too personal.

Personal stories are what appear in this volume. They are stories of visions or experiences that have invaded the lives of various people, all of whom are sane and rational individuals— each one a respected member of society. In many cases, the time and place and the individual(s) are all named, as they wished. In other cases, the individual(s) have wished to retain their privacy. Often the owners of a certain building—a hotel or mansion, for example—did not want the story associated with them or their establishment. This has been respected and fictitious names and places have been substituted. Each story is based on fact. I wanted it that way, for I have a few facts of my own.

Besides my fascination with the Old West as it existed and continues to exist in various forms today, I have a decided stake in taking interest in and investigating ghostly phenomena. In fact, it was a personal experience that led me to conclude that completing this volume might somehow release some tension from my own subconscious.

A major experience for me occurred in late May of 1970, when I was attending college at Montana State University in Bozeman. At the end of the famed Bozeman Road, a gold trail to Montana mining camps of the 1860s and '70s, Bozeman and the surrounding area is rich in the history of the period. There are many old houses and log cabins in the mountains and foothills near Bozeman that were shelter and home to people of the last century. One such dwelling proved to be inhabited by someone or something from that distant past.

For a botany class, a girlfriend and I were collecting wild plants on a lonely hillside above the Gallatin River some distance from town. Along the river bottom was an old abandoned house. Having grown up on a ranch, I was experienced in exploring old farmsteads, deserted country dance halls, and other remnants of the past. As a boy, I had found nothing in any of these old dwellings but a few relics and knickknacks, rotting wood, and assorted bird nests. I had felt no unusual awareness. But this old house was different.

My girlfriend commented on the strange feelings she was getting from the house, and I had to agree with her. We spoke no more about it and finished up our plant collecting. At dusk we began the trip back to Bozeman. A short way down the road, my girlfriend broke off what she was saying in midsentence. We looked at each other, then turned to the backseat. We saw nothing, but both of us felt a presence back there—a strong presence that scared us.

The remainder of the trip was a mixture of confusion and near terror. Who or what was in the backseat and why was it there? Why wouldn't it go away? My girlfriend and I spoke very little, trying hard to breathe normally. Finally, the presence seemed to go away and we relaxed. I dropped her off at her dormitory and parked my car. Later, in my own dorm, whatever it was came back.

It was late and I had just gotten into bed. I was lying on my stomach with my pillow curled up under my head, nearly asleep, when I felt something enter the room. Now I was wide awake. Then I felt the edge of my bed settling, as if someone had just sat down. I couldn't move; fear had petrified me. My arms and legs, my whole body, seemed numbed with shock. I couldn't make my mouth move even to yell.

Finally, after what seemed an intolerably long time, the pressure on the edge of my bed lessened and the feeling in the room dissipated. My nervous system settled down some. I turned over and looked through the darkness. I saw nothing. Whatever had been there was gone. After considerable time I fell asleep. I've often wondered who or what it was that wanted so badly to interact with me. Perhaps some day I'll learn the answer.

Since that time I have had other experiences, many of them while researching battlefields and lost trails for my novels. Late one foggy evening while driving alongside a pasture on the edge of Laurel, Montana, I noticed men standing among a herd of spotted horses. All of them wore feathers in their long hair. As soon as I slowed down to make certain of what I was seeing, the men vanished.

I have felt unseen presences, both good and bad, and have learned to be very respectful of all life, no matter what form it takes. I have been asked to help in discovering the reasons for peculiar hauntings or unusual circumstances, learning in the process that nothing is too far out of the ordinary.

On one occasion a professor from a Southern university, on vacation in the West, drove over a thousand miles to find me and ask how he might rid himself of a female spirit who had insisted on following him from a haunted hotel in New Mexico, riding all the way in his vehicle with both him *and* his girlfriend. I could plainly hear his disturbed voice over the phone, not far from where I lived, while he insisted that the spirit was in the phone booth with him, pinching him on the leg.

I believe everyone has a story, even if it is one that seems trite or inconsequential. We all have to link to those who came before us, and those with whom we interact as present family or loved ones. Often the connection continues even after death.

Now, whenever I hear somebody tell me a house is haunted or something unusual and inexplicable has occurred somewhere, I ask about it. This is, after all, where the Old West was—and still is. Things we cannot explain wander the ruins of the past.

Earl Murray
Ft. Collins, Colorado
May 1998

OLD FORTS
AND
BATTLEFIELDS

1

The Phantoms of Fort Laramie

**Fort Laramie National Historic Site
Fort Laramie, Wyoming**

From March of 1834 until March of 1890, Fort Laramie served as the hub of expansion into the Northwest. Wagon trains and other caravans on the major trails, including the California, the Oregon, and later the Bozeman, all passed the gates of what some historians have called the Queen of the Frontier Forts.

From its beginnings as an early fur-trading post until the last assembly of U.S. Army troops on the parade ground, this grand old fort saw every type of character who ever traveled into the vast frontier west of the Mississippi.

Today it is a national historic site, dedicated to the preservation and dissemination of history. Many people from all over the United States and the world visit the fort grounds annually to see the remnants of a faded but glorious past. Permanent staff members and summer intern workers give tours and relate the fort's history. And many of those who work there today, or who have worked there previously, will say the past may still exist within those walls. They say the old fort is still alive.

Retired ranger and caretaker Mike Caligiore worked at Fort Laramie from 1971 through 1985.

"After so many years out here, you see and hear all kinds of things," Caligiore related. "You don't say anything, because people would think you were batty, but I've seen them and so have others."

Caligiore remembers Quarters A, also known as the Captain's Quarters, to have an unusual presence within its walls. The two-story structure was built as a duplex, so that separate families could reside within the same building. Heavy doors were built in front and back on both sides of the duplex, and dead-bolt locks were installed to prevent entry from any direction.

As was Caligiore's duty, he would lock up Quarters A each night after the grounds were closed and the rounds were made. In the late fall and winter months the sun would be going down, or the landscape would be in total darkness. Visitors would be few at that time of year, and everyone working had little reason to remain after working hours.

On numerous occasions, Caligiore would be the last one left on the grounds. With his big flashlight, he would walk into Quarters A, often to meet with the inexplicable.

"I would walk through the front door on the east side," Caligiore remembers, "and then lock it behind me. I would go down the hallway to the back door and lock it. I then would go through the other side, from the back to the front, locking both doors behind me. But a lot of times I would come out the east side of the building to find a surprise. The first door would be unlocked and standing wide open."

Not only would the door be unlocked, but the heavy tumbler would be turned up as well. This became common. At first it confused Caligiore, then it startled him. He knew he was locking the doors as he went; he made a concerted effort to do so each time he made his rounds. It was obvious to Mike Caligiore that someone unseen was living in Quarters A.

The strange case of the unlocked doors grew to be more chilling to the caretaker. Noises upstairs on the second floor, or in the attic, would occur when he was making his rounds. Often the sounds could be heard in the daytime as well. But numerous investigations showed no one around, nor anything inanimate that might have fallen or tumbled down the stairs. Whoever was within the walls of Quarters A was invisible.

"One night it really got to me," Caligiore says. "I was making my rounds with my flashlight. I entered Quarters A and locked the front door of the first part of the building. Then I got ten feet from the back door and suddenly I felt someone grab me, slap me on the back. I swung the flashlight around real hard to hit whoever had grabbed me, and there was nothing there."

It happened several more times before Caligiore decided he had to do something about it, apart from reporting it. Who would believe him? It occurred to him to give the presence a name and see if he could communicate with whoever or whatever it was.

Caligiore named the ghost George.

"You might think I'm crazy, but I'd say to him, 'George, now if you want to go out or come in, you do it before I lock the door, okay? I have to keep these doors locked.' "

The approach seemed to work. Caligiore had less trouble keeping the doors locked after that. But it seemed that "George" would either forget or go back to his mischievous ways, and on occasion Caligiore would have to remind the spiritual presence about the doors.

The ghost in the Captain's Quarters seems to have an officer's personality. It appears to want control of the structure.

This was, and apparently still is, true of another one of the famous buildings on the grounds—a structure called Old Bedlam. Built in 1849 as quarters for bachelor officers, it became post headquarters. As such, Old Bedlam was no doubt the scene of many historic decisions involving Indian warfare and the escorting of the numerous wagon trains through hostile territory.

In 1863–64, Lieutenant Colonel William O. Collins commanded the fort. He and his wife lived on the second floor of the structure. During that period the building was the center of social life at the post, and the name Old Bedlam came into being. It is difficult to say whether it is Colonel Collins or some other ranking officer who makes an occasional appearance in Old Bedlam, but there is little doubt some eerie form of decision making is still being carried out here.

Two young women who worked there as summer help can remember the sunny afternoon in 1985 when they found themselves reunited with the dead.

They were sitting on the upper balcony of the building, talking and laughing. Suddenly there was a sharp rapping against the window directly behind them. Both girls turned to see the curtains drawn and the figure of a man in a cavalry officer's uniform looking out at them. "Be quiet!" he ordered. "We're having a meeting in here." Then he vanished before their eyes.

One of the young women sprained an ankle running down the stairs, but did not even feel the pain until at least a hundred yards away from Old Bedlam, where she collapsed and nearly went into shock.

"There are a lot of things that happen out there most people wouldn't believe," Caligiore says. "But when it happens to you, you know it's not your imagination."

Various persons among those who work or have worked

at the fort say that the cavalry barracks at times seem to have a life of their own. When it happens it is usually at dawn. You can hear the sounds of heavy tromping on the wooden board-walks—as if a number of heavy boots were running along, in a hurry to get someplace. The sounds can end as suddenly as they begin.

Those who have heard the noise wonder if it isn't the sound of ghost soldiers answering reveille. The sound is un-mistakable, they say—the heavy tromping, almost thundering on the old boardwalk. But the listener can only stare at an old, empty building.

Encounters with whatever it is from the past that remains behind at Fort Laramie are not limited to the employees. Some visitors have felt something at a particular place on the grounds, something they likely will never be able to explain.

Many visitors come to Fort Laramie on a yearly basis. Often they see or feel things and tell someone without ever leaving their name. One such visitor was a man educated in the care and psychological treatment of abused children. His visit to the fort left him visibly shaken and depressed.

"I got a very strong sensation while standing in the ruins of the old colonel's quarters," he told a tour guide. "I just know that some time in the distant past there had been some form of child abuse there. Just what I really don't know, but it was definitely child abuse. I didn't see or hear anything, but I certainly felt it."

There seems without question to be a lot of strong energy and emotion from the past that lingers in the ruins and even in the rebuilt sections of old Fort Laramie. Residents of the lit-tle town of Fort Laramie, and all along the old Oregon Trail, are aware of that.

It is also well known that Fort Laramie's phantom residents do not all exist within the fort grounds proper. In fact, the oldest ghost known to exist at this major historical site is one that reportedly can be seen riding a black horse every seven years—a woman in a green riding dress.

It is said that in 1871, Lieutenant James Nicholas Allison arrived at Fort Laramie from West Point to assume a cavalry command. He was well known and liked among the officers and immediately became part of the social structure at the fort.

A favorite pastime was wolf hunting, and Lieutenant Allison was asked to join one of the afternoon chases. Allison, who took his dog along, and the other hunters spread out over the wide rolling plains beyond the fort.

Late in the afternoon Allison found himself separated from the main group and decided to return to the fort. While riding back across a long hill, Allison saw a woman in a green dress on a black stallion traveling below him along the old Oregon Trail. She appeared to have long hair that was pinned up under a hat, with a black veil down over her face.

Allison, taken by surprise, could not understand why a woman would be riding way out there all alone. He didn't recognize her as being from the fort. He could see, though, that she was riding the black stallion at a run, and it occurred to the lieutenant that she might be in danger. He immediately gave chase.

Though Allison called out and tried to catch up to her, the woman kicked her horse all the harder and used a jeweled riding crop on its flank to outdistance Allison's horse. Allison hadn't noticed that his dog did not give chase with him but remained behind—pacing around and whining. Allison continued to pursue the young woman. But she was too far ahead and disappeared over the hill. A puzzled Allison rode to the summit, trying to understand why she hadn't stopped. He looked across the vast Wyoming plains in all directions. There was only the continuous wind and nothing else. There was no woman on a black horse to be seen anywhere. What bothered him even more was the absence of tracks on the trail. There was only unsettled dust.

Lieutenant Allison began to feel odd, wondering if he had actually seen the woman or not. Nothing at this point indicated there had ever been a woman in green on horseback. Finally he rode back down to where his dog stood whining, waiting for him. Allison's amazement turned to alarm; the dog was also visibly shaken. The lieutenant began to wonder if he hadn't just seen a ghost. He had no other way of explaining it.

When Allison returned to the fort, the other officers asked him what had kept him. They had become worried and were about to go out looking for him. The lieutenant hesitated at first, but finally shrugged and told them about the young woman in the green riding dress who wouldn't let him approach her.

"The Woman in Green," one of the older officers said. He was nodding, watching Allison's expression. "She's a ghost that rides out there," the older officer added. "Every seven years she rides. That don't mean your luck will turn bad, though."

Lieutenant Allison was somewhat relieved at the news, glad to know he hadn't lost his sanity. Yet the vision bothered him. He learned that the legend of the Woman in Green reached back at least twenty years before his arrival. The story was that the young woman had been an officer's daughter, brought out when the fort changed over from a fur-trading post to a military cantonment. The stories varied some, but it was thought the officer's daughter had wanted to marry someone he didn't want her marrying, and she had become angry and hard to manage.

She was prone to riding out from the fort against her father's wishes. It was during one of those rides that she never returned. She was never found, and until some of the neighboring Sioux clans and tribal bands began to tell stories of a *Wasicun* woman in green on a black horse who disappears, no one knew the fate of the officer's daughter. She had obviously died or been killed, and had felt compelled to ride that black horse somewhere—even in death.

From the time of the Woman in Green until the present, the impressions of the past have been strong at Old Fort Laramie. Located just off I-25 in the remote plains of southern Wyoming, the fort shows evidence that the Old West still lives here along with the New West. And those who have felt and seen the fort's past will always know that the remains of one of the West's most important military posts will always tell its stories in one form or another—and often from the lips of the dead.

2

Visions of
Reno Crossing

Little Bighorn Battlefield National Monument
Crow Agency, Montana

Though quite interesting, the site of the Battle of the Little
Bighorn is a tragic place. American Indians call this place the
Greasy Grass. On a hot Sunday in June 1876, Lieutenant
Colonel George Armstrong Custer and those in his detach-
ment met a large force of Indian warriors here, mostly Sioux
and Cheyenne. Custer and his men were wiped out to the
last man.

While Custer was meeting his fate, a battalion of soldiers
under the command of Major Marcus Reno fought on an
adjacent battlefield some five miles distant. Their fight lasted
through that day and into the next. Reno, who actually initi-
ated the fighting, was subsequently joined by a command
under Captain Frederick Benteen, but not before a great number of his men were cut down in a disorderly retreat across the
Little Bighorn River and into the surrounding hills.

The crossing on the Little Bighorn where Reno and his

men fled the Indian forces, hauling what dead and wounded they could carry with them, is now referred to as the Reno Crossing. On that day it was a scene of madness and blood. Now it stands as silent as infamous Last Stand Hill, where it is said that Custer and what remained of his men were finished off by the Indians.

The Indians also suffered the loss of many warriors that day, as well as some women and children. The shock of death hit both sides. To this day, the feel of loss and sorrow has never left the valley.

Though history has seen more monumental battles, the Little Bighorn fight provoked more than its share of discussion. The documented knowledge of the battle continues to increase. Troop and Indian movements throughout the encounter are now better understood. But history will forever hold to herself some of the secrets of that terrible day, for the dead cannot speak . . . or can they?

Christine Hope will always remember her small apartment near the battlefield cemetery. She will never fully understand what happened to her one night in the darkness of that apartment. After that unusual night, which was followed by a day of questioning her sanity, Chris Hope became a believer in the unexplained.

Chris was a student intern at the battlefield during the summer season of 1983. A native of Minnesota and not long out of college, she had come to the battlefield for a change of pace from social work. Tours and talks and seminars were soon a part of her daily routine; she enjoyed her work.

Toward the end of the season, Chris and a park ranger named Tim Bernardis decided they would visit that section of the battlefield known as the Reno Crossing. It was late in the evening and the excursion was planned for the afternoon of the following day.

Chris fell asleep on the sofa in her apartment that night.

Some time after midnight she awakened for some reason and began to look around the room. It was pitch-black, with only a shaft of moonlight coming in through a window across from the couch. When Chris looked more closely, she could see that the shaft of moonlight bathed a man's face, a man she did not know, who was sitting in one of her living room chairs.

She was immediately confused and frightened. Who was this man and how did he get into her apartment? And what did he want with her? He appeared to be dressed in a form of contemporary clothing, but something about him told Chris he was not a man from modern times. His hair was cut differently from the style she was used to seeing on most men. It alarmed her to realize that the haircut was more in style with the photos she had seen of soldiers who had fought in the Battle of the Little Bighorn.

Chris Hope remembered a lot of things about this intruder. She remembered his light beard and his flowing handlebar mustache. But what reached the deepest into her brain was his face, and the look in his eyes.

"It was his eyes that got to me the most," Chris said later. "It's hard to explain, but those eyes stood out. They were filled with incredible fright. The moon shone on them and they were filled with terror."

Chris could not believe she was actually seeing what was before her. The vision numbed her. Finally she blinked. When she refocused her eyes, the chair was empty.

The darkness seemed to close in now like an immense wall. What else might come out of this black space all around her? It was some time before Chris could move. She finally got to a light switch and flooded the room with light, then turned on the rest of the lights in the apartment. She was alone. There was no one to talk to, to ask if she had been dreaming. But Chris Hope knew when she was awake and when she was dreaming. She had certainly been awake.

When the first light finally entered the apartment, Chris got ready for another day of work. She tried to dispel from her mind what she had seen in the moonlight a few hours before. She looked closely at the chair next to the window. There was nothing about it on this bright fall morning to suggest that anything unusual had occurred the night before. But the vision of the man with the handlebar mustache remained like an indelible inset within her mind, his wide, terror-filled eyes staring at her.

All during that day, Chris kept feeling that those eyes were trying to convey a message. Something behind the unspeakable horror was reaching out to say something. She went about her schedule, her mind drifting at times to what had happened. Finally, she resolved to forget it in whatever way she could.

Around four o'clock that afternoon Chris and Tim Bernardis took their trip to the deep ravines that marked the area where Major Marcus Reno and his troops had fled in retreat from the oncoming warriors. Tim told Chris how the battle had begun at the eastern edge of the Indian encampment, and how, overpowered by overwhelming numbers, Reno turned tail for the cover of the trees along the river. During the fighting, Reno lost control of his command, and the soldiers scrambled through the water and into the hills beyond. Tim pointed out where various segments of the force, dragging what dead and wounded they could take with them, finally dug in and made a desperate stand.

At the bottom of a steep hill, near the edge of the Little Bighorn River, Chris noticed a solitary marker. A soldier had fallen here, Tim explained, one of Reno's men. The particulars about the man could be researched later in the files.

When their tour of the river crossing was complete, Chris and Tim went to the visitors' center. There Tim found a book published some years back and now out of print that detailed the military biographies of the men who died at the battle. The marker at the edge of the river belonged to a soldier who had been assigned to Company B of the Seventh Cavalry. His name was Second Lieutenant Benjamin H. Hodgson.

"Here is his picture," Tim said.

Chris looked and her breath stopped. The man had a long, flowing handlebar mustache. There was no question, she realized, that the photo was of the man she had seen in her apartment the night before.

"What's the matter?" Tim asked.

"You won't believe me," Chris said.

Tim persisted and Chris finally told him what had happened in her apartment the night before. Tim knew Chris to be levelheaded. She never spoke much about unusual things of any kind, let alone ghosts.

"Are you sure?" he asked her.

Chris nodded. She went over her experience, point by point, dwelling on the illuminated eyes that seemed to brim over with unspeakable horror. And as she spoke, it occurred to her that the eyes had been conveying the message that what had happened on that hot June day in 1876 should never have to happen to any human being of any race, and that death in such numbers on both sides, so swift and so terrible, was so tragic that no amount of reverence and respect would ever really suffice.

It occurred to Tim that one soldier who would have known the horror of dying during Reno's retreat was Second Lieutenant Benjamin Hodgson. Everyone in the regiment called him "Benny" and he was well known and liked by Reno's men. Hodgson was Reno's adjutant, as well as his friend. Hodgson died a frantic and drawn-out death at Reno Crossing.

Reno and his command had come under heavy fire from Indian rifles at the crossing. While Hodgson forded the river, his leg was shattered by a bullet that killed his horse. Fighting shock, he managed to grab a stirrup kicked out to him by another soldier. Hodgson was then dragged through the water to the opposite shore.

With his shattered leg he somehow managed to crawl partway up a steep bank before he was shot and killed by another Indian rifleman. His body rolled down the bank and came to rest near the water.

The story of Hodgson's appearance to Chris Hope made the rounds among employees at the battlefield. No one was especially surprised, for phantoms of unidentified soldiers had been seen off and on over the years in the apartments, as well as in a structure at the edge of the battlefield cemetery.

The mysterious stone house has been the site for a number of unusual stories, mostly of soldiers who are seen climbing the stairs. Chris Hope's story of Benjamin Hodgson was not out of place. In fact, one man stepped forward and confessed he himself had seen Hodgson a few years before, but only the soldier's head—in a white gaseous cloud—which had hovered over his bed in the middle of the night. The sighting had been under similar circumstances: just before a trip to the Reno Crossing.

Not long after her experience, Chris Hope's summer work at the battlefield came to a close. Besides memories of the sweeping hills and of the softly flowing river that passes through the valley, she will always feel the significance of that tragic day more than most people. She can never forget the face of that terrified soldier who came to her out of nowhere and taught her what the horror of battle is all about.

But Chris Hope and the others at the battlefield are not the only ones to have touched the distant past. Theirs could be called impromptu experiences, the significance of which is usually impossible to ascertain. But there are those who can hold history in their hand, literally, and have it speak to them.

A somewhat controversial approach to divining the hidden records of the past is a process called psychometry. This is a procedure that brings individuals with psychic powers (psychics) together with inanimate objects once owned or used by people having long since died. Certain of those psychics have the ability to "pick up on" or "feel" vibrations emitted by such objects. These individuals, evidence is beginning to show, can see into the lives of the dead.

The theory of how this might happen stems from a law of physics: all living things give off electromagnetic impulses, or vibrations—psychic traces that are left behind even after death. These unseen force fields are often referred to as imprints. Such imprints are transferred, especially during a state of intense emotion, from the personality of the living being to an inanimate object. These imprints apparently remain attached to the inanimate object indefinitely.

The imprints, according to psychics, reveal themselves to people who can read them much the same as motion-picture film on a screen; the psychic's mind is the screen upon which the imprints are projected. The imprints are not as clear as film, and are caught only in fragments, but they do present a series of images that can be interpreted by the psychic's mind and conveyed through normal conversation.

Old spurs, boots, rifles, arrows, empty cartridge casings, and similar artifacts carry imprints. For certain psychic people, these imprints have the potential to unlock secrets from the historic past.

From 1979 to 1981 a series of experiments in psychometry as it relates to history began under the direction of historian Don G. Rickey Jr., professor and author of the acclaimed book *Forty Miles a Day on Beans and Hay: The Enlisted Soldier Fighting the Indian Wars.* With the assistance of psychic Howard

R. Starkel, Dr. Rickey conducted an exploratory session and
subsequent experimental sessions to assess Starkel's ability to
unlock imprints of the past. Dr. Rickey's point of interest was
the site of the Battle of the Little Bighorn in June of 1876.

It's noteworthy that at the time Starkel had no background
in the events that took place at the Little Bighorn in 1876. In
fact, the psychic showed little knowledge of any type of Indian
war history. Questions during the sessions that might have
seemed trite to historians built an even bigger case against the
possibility of Starkel using his imagination to build upon
something he already knew a great deal about. Starkel knew
absolutely nothing about the country around the Little
Bighorn River, much less the documented facts about the
battle itself.

Following the initial exploratory sessions, another se-
quence of sessions took place in 1981 at the Little Bighorn
Battlefield National Monument. In attendance during the sessions in the basement of the visitors' center was James Court,
superintendent at the time, and Neil Mangum, who held the
position of historian at the battlefield.

Dr. Rickey published the results of the sessions, with input
from Neil Mangum. Segments of both sessions appeared in
The Courier, a National Park Service publication, and subsequently in somewhat altered form in *Applied PSI,* Volume
5, No. 1, Spring 1986. With appreciation to both authors
and publications, selected portions of the published reports
appear here.

The initial exploratory session took place in July 1979 in
Denver. Starkel was given a spur found on or near the battlefield. The artifact had been discarded some twenty years earlier from the museum collection. It was an iron spur, not an
1876 army brass spur of the type issued to the troopers as
standard equipment. Therefore, it was not considered to have
been an artifact associated with the conflict. Dr. Rickey saved

the spur literally from a garbage heap and added it to his own collection.

Indeed, some twenty years later, the spur was found to contain some unexplained form of energy. In the hands of Starkel the spur proved to be a link with a man who had died at Reno Crossing.

During one of the sessions in Denver, Dr. Rickey handed the spur to Starkel and told him nothing at all about it, not even where it had come from. After concentrating for five to ten seconds, Starkel began to speak. His words, in part, were as follows:

> I was hurt; this was found in a desolate area; I am with other people. . . . Trees were nearby, in a valley . . . there is emotion . . . hurry, startled, want to get on horseback, close to a stream, where all my activity is starting, trying to get to horseback. I am hurt and want to get across the stream to a hill to defend myself, about 150 yards away from the stream. I want to take off a black boot. . . . I think I was shot, and am in pain but still running. . . .
>
> We're just a group, but not a big group. Attackers pulled back. I am crossing the stream with a few others. The larger group is elsewhere. I am a big man, but have no hat. The people chasing me . . . one has a bull's eye painted on his chest—they are mounted. I feel directionally disoriented. I go across the stream . . . this spur was lost on the south side just after I crossed the stream to climb the high ridges, in a panic to leave. I want to go across the river and north, to a main body, but can't. . . .
>
> The enemies have backed away; they don't have time to play with us. They go back to fight the main body going to the northwest. Horses lost at the river. I see a fire away from the object. The owner did not make it through the battle.

There was little question in Dr. Rickey's mind that Starkel had been talking about Reno's retreat. The description of the terrain, especially the fighting in the trees and subsequent dash across the river for the bluffs, was more than enough information to seal the fact that Starkel was seeing, through the iron spur, the Reno fight as it took place more than a hundred years before.

In addition, Starkel stated that he saw a fire. Historical records indicate that the grass along the valley floor was set ablaze by the warring Indians as they left the scene of battle on the evening of June 26.

The information about the individual who had worn the iron spur during the conflict proved even more startling. Riding with Reno's battalion was a contract surgeon named J. M. DeWolf, who was wounded and killed after crossing the river. DeWolf was a civilian and therefore had to outfit himself; he likely chose the more common iron spurs over the military pattern brass spurs worn by the soldiers.

The marker where J. M. DeWolf fell is located close to the top of a ridge above the river, where he died while trying to reach the defensive position.

Neil Magnum, the present superintendant, was the battlefield historian at the time. He was awestruck by the impressions brought forth during the sessions with Starkel. "Coming from a man who had never seen the country and knew little about the battle," Magnum says, "the information was amazingly accurate. It seemed impossible to me that any of it could be contrived."

While reading and gathering various artifacts—primarily spent cartridge shells of different calibers and makes—Mangum became involved in the sessions himself. He was startled to see that time after time Starkel came close to describing exactly where the artifact had been found.

"Mr. Starkel was not well versed in historic military weaponry and showed as much on various occasions," Mangum said. "When given a Spencer cartridge and asked to read the imprint from it, Mr. Starkel discussed how the user had loaded it during the battle from the butt end of the rifle, as the weapon was designed to be loaded. Knowing something about ordinary firearms and their design, Mr. Starkel then asked, 'How could this be?' "

As the session progressed, Starkel was given a .50-caliber Martin-primed army shell case. Starkel read the psychic imprint on the shell case, in part, as follows:

> The user was a hostile [Indian] . . . kneeling and shooting—not too far from water. . . . The user feels very angry, hostile toward the soldiers. . . . The user is not rapid-firing—he doesn't have much ammunition—a careful user of ammunition. He accounted for three soldiers here—he wasn't more than fifty, sixty yards from the soldiers, and other Indians are up closer to the soldiers—some mounted. He was a marksman, but the recoil hurt his shoulder. . . .
>
> He has long leggings on, no feathers I can see . . . hair divided into three braids. Firing his weapon, there is something like a back blast—it is not like a Springfield carbine. . . .
>
> I feel his wife was killed in the recent past, and he blames the army for this—south and a little west, a long distance. Several women were killed there, in a mountainous area, with backs to some cliffs, at least one and a half years before. . . .
>
> At one point a lot of Indians leave the fighting area

and go northward. But the shell user stays in the same place or area, and is still there at the end. The shell user walks away when the shooting stops, he is looking over his own casualties—scattered. Some scavenging is going on, for weapons and ammunition. An occasional shot is heard. He went through the saddlebags on a dead horse. . . . His shoulder is sore from shooting. The battle was not long, but it was intense.

Even in the present time, the battle appears to still rage. It is impossible to predict on what given day or under what conditions, but there seems to be a strong turmoil still present.

In August 1986, Thelma Hargrove of Billings, Montana, and her daughter, Cody, were entertaining friends from Washington State. They decided to visit the battlefield and after viewing Last Stand Hill, drove out to the Reno-Benteen site.

"It was a hot afternoon and very still," Thelma remembers. "I thought it unusual that we were the only people in the parking lot. Cody and our friends left the car to walk on the footpaths but because I have a bad knee, I stayed inside the car and waited."

Not long after Cody and the others had left, an odd feeling came over Thelma; a cold, foreboding sensation.

"A strange wind came up and I began to hear noise and yelling. I heard Indians and horses and shooting, right outside the car. I couldn't see anything, but I got so frightened I couldn't move."

The sound of battle lasted nearly ten minutes, at which time Cody returned to the car and mentioned she had heard shots and shouts, and wondered if there was a reenactment going on somewhere.

"I think it was the real thing," Thelma told her. "It's time to go home."

Equally strange was the experience of Joyce Thierer on a

hot summer day in 1984. Joyce was employed as a seasonal worker and was mending a fence along the battlefield boundary to stop neighboring cattle from wandering onto the battlefield to graze. She was busy tightening the wire and hammering staples in place when she saw something develop along the slopes below her.

"It was a strange fog and it was filled with the sounds of yelling and shooting," she remembers. "And the most disturbing of all was the horses. The smell was so strong."

All animals give off a pungent odor when extremely afraid and that afternoon, the air was filled with the smell of terrified horses.

"It was all coming up the draw toward me and I scrambled up the slope as fast as I could, carrying all my gear with me. When I got to the top, I collapsed on my back. I felt cold, even though the temperature was well over a hundred degrees that day."

After a few minutes and still not fully recovered from the incident, Joyce radioed in that she was through for the day. Her boss asked her if she was sick and she replied that she wasn't, nor had she seen any rattlesnakes. She just felt that it was time to come in.

At the visitors' center, she was met by Mardelle Plainfeather, an employee who had herself seen a vision of men on horseback a few years before—Indian warriors who disappeared over the hill into the sunset when she went to look for them. She could tell by the look on Joyce's face that she had experienced something very unusual.

"Did something happen out there?" Mardelle asked.

Joyce told her story, and Mardelle said that she wasn't the only one who had experienced something unusual on that part of the battlefield. Mardelle then asked her if she wanted to sign the register of those who had witnessed Reno's retreat.

The valley of the Greasy Grass, the Little Bighorn, remains untouched from the time of the infamous battle that will never rest. The visitor can feel the sense of emotion here, not merely because there is much to document the dead, but because the ground is sacred. Anyone with normal human emotions can't help but sense the feelings that linger here.

Together with the spirits that linger near Reno Crossing, or make their way to the apartments and the old stone house at the cemetery, there are inanimate pieces of the past scattered throughout the valley that will never rest. As much as those wandering phantoms of dead men, these artifacts lie buried with secrets that may someday be uncovered.

Perhaps the spirits who know those artifacts as their own will tell their horrible stories to someone who can feel them, and the faces of the past will come into view once again.

3

The Hill at
Hat Creek

Hat Creek (Warbonnet Creek) State Historic Site
Northwestern Nebraska

Dressing in period costume and going on outings has become, for a number of historians, a popular means of researching a particular time or a series of events. It is called professional living history. The Indian wars period is as popular and interesting as any other segment of our nation's past, and there are many who organize meetings and encampments each year designed to reenact that frontier period. Men come in the military dress of that era; women come attired as frontier emigrants and army wives.

These journeys into frontier history can enlighten those who want the feel of the past. It enables them to have a sense of falling back in time, which accompanies living out-of-doors, or in historic buildings and sites where nothing has changed but the hundred or more years on the calendar.

Often such experiences bring on the past in ways that are inexplicable. John Grant and Lester Barton are two close friends associated with a university history department. For these two men a peculiar night in September 1984 at the Hat Creek battlefield in Nebraska brought them closer to the past than they had ever before dreamed possible.

Nightfall was complete on the fourth day of their encampment, and the sky had filled with dark clouds. Dry lightning was striking a distance from where the rows of white canvas tents formed the bivouac of the Fifth Cavalry. For John Grant, everything seemed to be just as it had been during the height of the Indian wars on the Plains. The setting resembled a military campaign against the Cheyenne Indians—the troops encamped for the night, while the rolling plains reached out endlessly in all directions.

Grant was sitting at the top of the hill, the monument to his back. He was guarding the camp, as the midnight-to-two watch was his. He had his overcoat buttoned up tightly against the oncoming storm.

"The view was rather spectacular," Grant told friends later. "The moon would come and go behind the clouds, and the entire horizon would light up. But there was no smell of rain in the air—just wind, black clouds, and lightning."

The wind through the grass on the ridge became a backdrop to Grant's thoughts on the upcoming academic year and other private matters. He was just passing time, waiting for two o'clock, when he could go back down the hill and wake up the relief guard.

It was then that he heard voices—the sound of men whispering to one another. It was jumbled and impossible to understand clearly, but it was definitely men's voices.

Grant strained to hear, but the sounds died out. He at first dismissed the whispering as his imagination. But the voices started again, louder than before. And now he could hear footsteps, the *swish-swish* of feet parting the prairie grass. It seemed as if the men were very close to him now.

Grant smiled. He decided it was likely the first sergeant or the corporal of the guard sneaking up on him to make sure he was awake and on duty. Grant got up and began to walk around the hill. Lightning flashed, revealing only empty prairie around him. There were no trees or brush anywhere, and Grant knew no one could possibly get close enough for him to hear him without being visible. He began to get nervous.

He looked down on the tents below, white blotches in neat rows, as lightning and intermittent moonlight splashed through the darkness. He now realized beyond any doubt that he was the only one on the hill, that everyone else was below sleeping.

He went back to his position and sat down. He placed a round of ammunition into his .45-70 Springfield rifle and strained to hear as he again heard the muffled, whispering voices. Then he felt a strong presence that sent tingles through him and made his hair stand on end. He turned around to look at the monument and sat paralyzed.

A cloud of greenish mist was boiling just off the ground. It swirled and moved slowly along the side of the monument. There was no real shape to the cloud, but it continued to move around the monument.

Grant managed to get up. He started to walk, then ran down the hill toward the encampment. There were thirty minutes left on his watch, but John Grant wanted nothing more to do with the hill.

Lester Barton took his watch just after Grant came down off the hill. Grant said nothing to Barton about what he had experienced. It was not until a couple of months later, when the two men were sitting in a lounge near their university campus, that they began to reflect upon the hill above Hat Creek.

"Did anything funny happen to you up on that hill that night?" Grant asked Barton.

Barton looked at Grant a moment before he answered.

"You mean you saw something too? And heard voices?"

Grant nodded.

"Why didn't you tell me?" Barton asked. "I just about lost my mind up there that night."

"I didn't want to talk about it," Grant said. "I was afraid you would think I was crazy. I thought I was crazy myself at the time."

The history of the hill above Hat Creek is one drenched in Cheyenne Indian blood. Shortly after the death of Custer and his men at the Little Bighorn, news of the battle reached the reservation at Red Cloud Agency. Within a short time a number of warring Cheyenne took their horses and started north for the Black Hills.

The Fifth U.S. Cavalry, under General Wesley Merritt, had been ordered to cut off the advancing Cheyenne forces and return them to the reservation. Merritt's chief of scouts was William F. Cody, later to be known as Buffalo Bill. He was dressed lavishly in a Mexican suit of black and scarlet velvet, trimmed with silver buttons and lace. He appeared to be presenting himself for the theater, as one soldier who kept a diary of the campaign noted.

In mid-July of 1876, a month after Battle of the Little Bighorn, Merritt's forces met and defeated the contingent of Cheyenne at Hat Creek. Much of the fight took place on horseback, and though the Cheyenne were noted horsemen and fighters, they were outnumbered that day. The warriors were also poorly armed and weak for lack of nourishing food.

During the fight, Cody fired his carbine at a Cheyenne named Yellow Hand. The bullet passed through Yellow Hand's leg and killed his pony. Cody then finished off the wounded warrior.

Cody removed the Cheyenne's war bonnet and weapons, which he later used in some of his theatrical shows. After he escorted Merritt's command and the defeated warriors back to the reservation, Cody was looked upon with awe by the Cheyenne remaining at the agency. His medicine must have been powerful to kill the warrior Yellow Hand.

The site of the battle was Warbonnet Creek, later renamed Hat Creek. History also tells us that Cody went on to become a legendary figure and that the Cheyenne, along with the other Plains tribes, lost many of their people in battle. What cannot be documented is what remains at Hat Creek so many years after the fighting.

Nothing will ever prove that John Grant and Lester Barton had their strange experiences on the hill above the Hat Creek battleground. But the two men will never have to be convinced that there was something there—something that has yet to be explained by modern science.

Grant and Barton have discussed similar experiences with other members of historical reenactment groups. Many of them have had paranormal encounters with those who possibly fought and died on the various battlefields throughout the West. It is a situation not often talked about outside of friendly circles. Credibility among historians is accumulated through time and hard work; spreading unsubstantiated campfire tales can harm a solid position.

But among those whose senses have picked up something they can't entirely understand, credibility has taken on deeper meaning: it is believed by some of these individuals that removing all ties to the contemporary—such as modern clothing, jewelry, and other accessories—and dressing entirely in period costume, might possibly call something up from that past to which they are striving so hard to relate.

If this is true, it could then be deduced that the dead from another dimension recognize the clothing or possibly the psychic condition of the reenactors. For it has been demonstrated that reenacting the past can sensitize the mind into feeling the past.

The Hat Creek incident is only one of many that have been reported during reenactment exercises at various forts and battlefields around the West. The men and women who participate have come to know paranormal situations as almost commonplace. The creaks and groans of old fort buildings, or the wind sweeping the High Plains hilltops, are not sufficient explanation. Swamp gas is a rare commodity in these semiarid reaches of cactus and sagebrush. There is much more to it than anything now scientifically known, say those who have had the experiences.

Those who go to great lengths do succeed in getting into the period of time they wish to explore. The individual who dresses in buckskins, leaves his watch and rings behind, and rides a horse into the high Rocky Mountains most certainly will learn what it was like to be a mountain man. Similarly, those who wear cavalry uniforms and march or ride into the open country, subsisting on beans and hardtack, will undoubtedly feel what a nineteenth-century soldier must have felt. That is what reenactment is all about.

But it appears they may see and feel more than initially expected. For among the ranks, soldiers have been seen that nobody can recognize—soldiers once dead who have come back to march again.

4

The Blue Light Lady

Fort Hays State Historic Site
Hays, Kansas

Where the wind once swept across the vast Kansas prairie, civilization has now made its mark. Today towns and farms cover the expanses where tall grasses once served as the food source for vast buffalo herds. A major interstate now crosses the plain where wagon trains of emigrants used to make their slow progress toward a new life.

But there are many in the town of Hays in west-central Kansas who are convinced the historic past may be alive yet—and capable of alarming manifestations.

Mark Gilbert is not a Kansan, but he encountered a segment of Kansas history that will remain in his mind throughout his life. He will never understand a midsummer's evening he spent working on the outskirts of Hays.

Gilbert, a Texan, was just over twenty years old at the time. He was working as a combine operator for a custom cutting contractor, a business in which combiners work for a fee to harvest a farmer's grain.

It was the second week in July, as Gilbert remembers. The wheat fields in central Kansas were gold and ready for harvest. A few days before, Gilbert's boss had agreed to cut wheat owned by the university system in Hays. Now they were finishing that job. Then they would be moving to the north to harvest near the state line.

It was the last day of their work just south of Hays. A curiously red sunset, very windy, streaked the western sky in crimson. Gilbert's boss was in a hurry to finish the cutting, ready to continue into the night, if necessary. There were four combines going on two fields, as Gilbert remembers, and as the other three combines finished, he continued to work. There was little wheat left to harvest in the field Gilbert was working, and he decided to finish the job with his combine lights on, while the other workers called it a day.

The red sunset faded to twilight. Gilbert's boss left a grain truck at the edge of the field, so the worker could empty the wheat into it when he was finished. Gilbert told his boss and the other workers he would join them in town for supper and a few beers in about an hour.

In the deepening twilight, the wind died down considerably and Gilbert was glad for the sudden quiet. During the day the blowing grain dust had filled his eyes, and they hurt. But he had washed them out with water from his water bag. He felt better now that the end of the harvest was in sight.

He worked with the radio in the combine cab playing, and watched the wheat flow into the sickle, or cutting bar, of the combine. It became a scene that played over and over in front of his eyes. In the darkness, the stalks of wheat cast odd shadows.

He turned a corner to make what would be the next-to-last round in the field. At the edge of the wheat was the outline of the grain truck. He remembered looking over at it and then back, then suddenly stepping on the combine's brakes. Crossing in front of the machine, in the shadows just beyond the lights, was what appeared to be a woman in a long blue dress.

"It was a woman and it didn't seem like she was walking normally," Gilbert recalls, "but kind of drifting. Actually, drifting pretty fast. In the lights I was sure the dress was blue. But then she was gone."

He looked all around the combine for any sign of the woman in the blue dress. He took a deep breath, trying to decide whether or not he had actually seen the figure. It had all happened in a few seconds.

After he was sure there was nobody around, Gilbert put the combine back into gear and started cutting again. He turned the radio off now, concentrating on where he was going and everything around him. He looked around constantly, his nerves on edge.

The darkness outside the cab of the combine seemed to be even blacker now. He considered stopping and going into town, but decided against it. Who would believe him? His boss might become angry. Gilbert had said he would finish cutting the field, and it would seem like he was just in a hurry to get to the bar. Besides, only part of a round remained. He had to finish.

He continued cutting the wheat. The lights of the combine showed the stalks of grain as they moved into the sickle, were cut off, and then threshed inside the combine. He was certain he was going to see the woman in the blue dress, and the fear caused him to tighten up inside. When a jackrabbit bounded from the wheat just in front of the lights, Gilbert thought his heart had stopped.

After the rabbit, he began to laugh at himself. Most likely he hadn't even seen a woman at all. It was probably some form

of strange shadow that the wheat and the combine lights had
caused. That was what he told himself.

He finished harvesting the field and steered the combine
over to the grain truck. He positioned the combine so that the
spout extended over the box of the truck. Then he began to
empty the hopper.

While the wheat spilled into the back of the truck, he
climbed down from the cab and got a shovel. He then returned to the back of the truck and began to spread the wheat
around to make room for the rest of the grain.

It was hard work and Gilbert broke into a sweat immediately. His thoughts now were on getting into town and show-
ering, then joining his boss and fellow workers. When the last
of the grain came out of the combine, he jumped down from
the truck and climbed back into the combine cab to turn off
the auger. Then he climbed back down.

It was still now, and a large part of the moon was shining,
just rising. Gilbert remembered that he had left the keys in the
combine and climbed up the ladder into the cab. Part way up
the ladder, he felt that someone was watching him from behind.

He turned and looked down. There was a strange and
hazy whitish-blue light on the ground at the foot of the ladder. Inside the light was the figure of a woman in a long blue
dress. Her face, partially covered by what appeared to be a
bonnet, was lifted to his. It was a face shrouded in cloudy
haze, as Gilbert recalled, but it was that of a woman.

He couldn't remember her features, whether she was
pretty or happy or sad, for in that split-second of recognition,
he turned away from the image and clung helplessly to the ladder. Traumatized, he couldn't speak or yell, or even move for
a time. When the feeling of the presence was finally gone, he
mustered up enough nerve to look down again.

There was only the dark ground below him, nothing to

show that anything had been there. But Mark Gilbert was sure of what he had seen—it would never leave his mind.

His hands trembled as he retrieved the key from the cab. Then he climbed back down, looking all around him while he ran to the truck. He drove into Hays to meet his boss and his friends, wondering what had happened and why. Who was the woman and why had she appeared to him?

Once in town and cleaned up, Gilbert resolved not to say anything to anybody. He didn't know the guys he was working with all that well yet, and he certainly didn't know this town. Just try to forget it, he told himself.

But he was changed somehow by what had happened; his fellow workers commented on how jumpy he seemed to be. He didn't drink much beer, and he remained in the company of somebody all the time. It led his boss to remark jokingly that he believed Gilbert had seen a ghost out in the field.

Everyone laughed but Gilbert.

The next morning, when they all went out to get the combines loaded onto flatbed trucks for the trip north, Gilbert looked across the stubble of the harvested field and shook his head. It seemed now like any normal wheat field he had ever combined in his life.

But it wasn't normal. Someone else was out there, he felt, someone possibly even at this moment, unseen. He didn't know who she was or why she was there, and he didn't want to ask. But come another nightfall—when they would all be gone north—Mark Gilbert believed that the woman in the bonnet and long blue dress would likely be drifting across the fields once again.

The mysterious woman who frightened Mark Gilbert during that summer night in 1977 is well known to the people of

Hays. Had he brought up the fact that he had seen something, he might have felt better.

The legend of Elizabeth Polly is one that will live forever in Ellis County. There is a park named after the pioneer woman who died at old Fort Hays back in 1867. Today a monument stands at the site of her interment at the summit of Sentinel Hill.

Her story is hard to trace through fort records, but solidly rooted in local lore. Once the site of Fort Hays, the military post during the Indian wars, the town of Hays, Kansas, will always think of Elizabeth Polly as the symbol of all that is just and good.

Taken as told, the Elizabeth Polly story is an inspiring one. It is said she traveled the Smoky Hill River country in the mid-1860s with her husband, Ephraim, a settler who supplied forts and outposts with dry goods. For a time they traveled the Fort Larned Trail, and the Fort Hays–Fort Dodge Trail, before finally settling at Fort Hays, where Elizabeth grew to love the wild plains.

She could often be seen taking walks outside the fort to the bluffs, which run to the south and west of the old fort grounds. She could be seen in the evenings, at sundown, walking the bluffs, her bonnet fastened tightly and her blue dress moving in the wind. It was a place she loved, a place where she could look out over the fort and then to the west, where the High Plains stretched out toward the distant Rocky Mountains. She would remain there until nightfall settled over the vast plains, and then return to the fort. She had mentioned frequently that when she died, these bluffs were to be her eternal home.

Old Fort Hays records document an Ephraim Polly who was a hospital steward there during an outbreak of cholera in 1867. Elizabeth, though not mentioned in the records, went on to win her place in local and regional history.

During the cholera epidemic, she became the angel of the fort, comforting the soldiers in their illness. She was there whenever she was needed, and everyone came to know and love her. But in that summer of 1867, Elizabeth Polly contracted cholera while treating the dying.

On her deathbed she was assured the bluffs above the fort would be her final resting place. But it was found that the top, where she had walked so many evenings, was too rocky for a gravesite. So after a full military funeral, she was interred at the base of the bluffs.

Many of the soldiers at the fort were also interred near her at the military cemetery. But in December 1905 the bodies were ordered exhumed and were reburied at Fort Leavenworth. Elizabeth Polly's grave was left untouched until a reported reinterment took place in 1941. It is said that the Civilian Conservation Corps moved her remains to the top of the hill, where the monument to her legend stands today.

There are those who speculate as to why the phantom Blue Light Lady haunts the hills outside of Hays. One possible theory is that Elizabeth Polly cannot rest, that she is still in search of the soldiers who were buried with her and later moved. Others say that she loved those hills so much in life that she cannot make herself leave them in death.

Over the years, various newspaper and historical articles have told and retold the story of Elizabeth Polly—that she did and still does walk the bluffs. Those who go by actual record dispute that she was ever really there, even in life. But the monument at the site of the Lonely Grave—as it is known—maintains that she did exist, and that this remarkable woman lost her earthly life tending to sick and dying soldiers.

Mark Gilbert's experience with the phantom of Elizabeth Polly was preceded by a number of sightings, including one case that occurred some time just before 1960. A night patrolman with the Hays police force was cruising a newly constructed piece of roadway on the edge of town. It was around two-thirty in the morning and all was quiet. The patrolman was lost in his thoughts, until something strange and terrifying happened.

Bob Maxwell, associated with Fort Hays State University, was also a patrolman on duty that night. He remembered that odd night when he heard the other officer call for help over the radio.

"I responded to his call," Maxwell said recently, "and found him parked on the bypass, standing by his patrol car. He was chain-smoking and his face was white. He was pretty shook up. I asked him what was wrong and he told me that he thought he had run over a woman, but he couldn't find her."

The distraught officer then told Maxwell that he had been driving along slowly when a woman in a long blue dress, wearing what looked like a bonnet, suddenly appeared in his headlights. He had no time to stop. When he got out to see how badly she was hurt, there was no one there.

Maxwell didn't know what to tell him. They looked at each other a long time. Both knew of the Elizabeth Polly legend. Maxwell shrugged while the other officer shook his head and repeated over and over, "She was there. . . . I saw her, I tell you. . . . She was there. . . ."

One of the first recorded sightings of Elizabeth Polly was as far back as 1917. In that year a farmer named John Schmidt was on horseback early one morning, driving his cows from pasture into the barn for milking. His dog was with him, helping drive the cows. Schmidt, it is reported, noticed a woman wearing a blue dress and bonnet walking across the pasture. She was traveling from the direction of old Fort Hays toward an abandoned shack.

Puzzled, Schmidt called to her. There was no response. The dog trotted toward home, leaving Schmidt behind. Schmidt rode toward the woman but still could get no response. He gave up when his horse refused to take him close to the mysterious woman.

Schmidt returned to his farm, a short distance away, where his wife and kids stood watching. Schmidt could not tell his wife who the woman was and reported that the woman avoided any contact, by speech or eyesight. The woman had gone into the shack at the edge of the pasture.

After a day's work, Schmidt and his brother-in-law, Anton Rupp, returned to the shack to investigate. Schmidt's wife testified she had not seen the woman leave the shack all day, and supposed she had stayed there. Schmidt and Rupp found the shack vacated and filled with dust. There was no evidence anyone had ever been there.

While the legend of Elizabeth Polly lives on, there have been other, lesser-known incidents that suggest the spirits of old Fort Hays still exist within the town of Hays itself.

In 1902 the old officers' quarters were moved from the fort site into town, where they served as an apartment complex. In the early 1960s two unrelated but equally frightening experiences happened to college students living in the building.

After classes one afternoon a young woman returned to her apartment to see soldiers in full military dress sitting around her dining-room table playing cards. She turned and fled immediately. A few years later a young man named Adam, rooming with another college student on the second floor of the building, had an experience he will never forget.

Adam was sitting at his desk studying. His roommate was attending classes on campus at the time. The quiet in the building was broken by the sound of a door slamming downstairs. Adam then heard the sound of footsteps crossing the floor and approaching the stairs.

He naturally assumed his roommate had returned from

campus and was on his way up to the room. Adam continued studying. The footsteps came up the stairs and into the room. Adam turned but saw nobody there. He was shocked, for the sounds of the footsteps continued toward his roommate's bed.

Then Adam watched in terror as the edge of his roommate's bed sagged.

Dropping his books, Adam fled the room. He soon moved out, as did his roommate when he heard the story.

The old officers' quarters were returned to the fort site in May of 1987. Since then there have been no reported paranormal incidents. But part of the history of the U.S. Army is contained within those old walls, and the legacy of the soldiers will always exist.

But by far the best-known legend of Hays, Kansas, is the Blue Light Lady, Elizabeth Polly, who it seems must want to move from some unknown dimension into the world of flesh and blood. There are those who will always have her vision deep in their mind, for they have seen her. And there are those who might some day see her, wandering the fields and pastures around the Lonely Grave at the crest of Sentinel Hill.

OLD HOTELS
AND
MANSIONS

5

The Legacy of
Winchester Mansion

Winchester Mansion
San Jose, California

One of the country's largest—and possibly most eerie—residences is a 160-room Victorian mansion located in San Jose, California. The incredible structure covers more than six acres and took thirty-eight years to construct—all to appease the dead.

Behind it all was Sarah Winchester, a woman obsessed with escaping the deceased spirits of those killed by the infamous Winchester repeating rifle. This rifle was among the most widely used of all firearms during the period of the Indian wars and the westward movement. As a result, the deaths attributed to the gun are countless. And the heir to the fortune, Sarah Winchester, believed the dead were chasing her.

In the fall of 1862, Sarah married William Wirt Winchester, the son of the Honorable Fisher Winchester—the "Rifle King." Sarah was small and delicate, but vivacious. She was interested in the paranormal and delved into it to a considerable degree. It was when her only child, Annie Pardee, died within a month of birth that Sarah Winchester slowly but surely allowed her mind to slip into another dimension.

This was further compounded by the death of William Wirt from tuberculosis some fifteen years later. After that she spent almost all her time in bereavement for her lost husband and daughter and sought the help of a psychic and medium in Boston. This man said her husband was speaking through him and that she was to be warned of avenging spirits—those who had fallen to the Winchester rifle. They were after her, the medium said, and she was to sell her property in New Haven and journey with haste into the West. There she was to seek out and buy a mansion and sufficient property so that she could add on and build a huge dwelling to house the dead.

"You will know the house when you see it," the medium is reported to have told her. "Spend whatever you have to in order to make room for the spirits of those killed by the rifle."

Sarah Winchester headed west immediately with the conviction that should she not carry out the wishes of her dead husband the spirits would kill her.

Her journey took her to California, where in 1884 she found what she wanted near the Pacific Ocean. It was an eight-room house under construction, perfect in her mind for the plans that the dead wanted carried out. She immediately set carpenters to work day and night to add more rooms onto the mansion, to house those lost spirits and thereby placate them in some way.

An overwhelming project lay ahead for Mrs. Winchester. But she had inherited some twenty million dollars, so the cost meant nothing. Her staff eventually reached as many as twenty full-time carpenters, equally as many servants, and from twelve to eighteen gardeners to tend the expansive grounds. She had a large bell installed in a high gable to signal the beginning and end of the day. The bell could also be heard ringing during the night, when Sarah was supposedly communicating with the spirits of slain men, assuring them the construction of the mansion was continuing.

Sarah Winchester never let up in her quest to appease the many who had fallen to the rifle. She detailed how the rooms and additions were to be constructed. She made use of the number thirteen again and again: thirteen blue and amber stones in a spider-glass window; thirteen lights on the chandeliers; thirteen windows and doors in the sewing room; thirteen baths; thirteen cement blocks in the carriage entrance hall; thirteen hooks in her séance room; she even divided her will into thirteen parts and signed it thirteen times.

Sarah Winchester conceived many forms of construction angles to try to confuse the spirits that might be wandering the house in search of her. She had stairways built with thirteen steps that climbed to nowhere—dead ends into walls and ceilings. Some windows looked out onto walls, and one was built into the floor. Some doors led into blank walls, and railing posts were turned upside down.

Throughout the mansion she detailed the construction of numerous twisting corridors and secret passageways. In many places she had the walls sealed off so that no one could enter. She moved continuously throughout the day, overseeing the work, and slept in a different bedroom each night—so that the spirits would never know exactly where she was when darkness fell.

Though she lived in constant fear of her possible sudden demise, Sarah Winchester proved to be a remarkable innovator. There are those who say her genius can be credited to the spectral images she spoke of constantly as being her advisers. She seemed to be constantly ripping up constructed rooms and hallways to make them over into something different that she had somehow "received" during the previous night.

No matter the source of her inspiration, Sarah Winches-

ter built an architectural masterpiece that boasted the most
modern heating and sewer systems of the time, as well as
button-operated gas lights. There were three working elevators
and forty-seven fireplaces, though one was built to end just
before it reached the top of the ceiling. The fireplaces were
equipped with hinged drops for ashes and with concealed
firewood boxes. She was a pioneer in the use of wool for in-
sulation, and devised a window catch patterned after the Winchester rifle trigger and trip-hammer mechanism. She had a
tiltable floor constructed so that water dumped on it could be
made to pour out of a trap door and onto her garden below.
She was never at a loss for ideas.

The craftsmanship was of the finest and the materials the
best available. Often a single worker would be kept busy for a
year or more on a single project. Rare hardwoods were used
for hand-laid, parquet floors, while the doors were inlaid with
German silver and bronze. Gold and silver were used in the
chandeliers, and art-glass windows installed in the walls. Much
of this exquisite material was purchased through Tiffany's of
New York, as well as from various outlets across Europe, including crystal from Val Saint-Lambert in Belgium.

Rooms within the mansion were used to store rolls of
French wallpaper; stained-glass doors and windows, often with
jewels embedded in them; numerous paintings; and various
types and sizes of copper, bronze, gold, and silver ornaments.
These things awaited placement in the mansion's many rooms
under construction, while simultaneous shipments of more
furnishings and materials—including trainloads of stone—
awaited transport at railroad sidings and shipment points
throughout the area.

Her garden was constructed and maintained in much the
same paranoid fashion as the interior of the mansion. There
were many pathways that crossed the grounds and led to

nowhere, as well as numerous orchards with trees tightly planted to allow little room between—hiding places from which to observe the ever-pursuing dead.

Included among the ornaments in the garden was the statue of an Indian that Mrs. Winchester named Chief Little Fawn, who was erected to fire arrows at hidden enemies in the shrubbery. Chief Little Fawn, Sarah Winchester believed, might in time help her atone for many Indian deaths attributed to the Winchester rifle.

There seemed never to be a moment when Sarah Winchester wasn't thinking of the dead, whether inside or outside her mansion. As she grew more reclusive, most of her time was spent indoors, where she made every effort to console those killed by the terrible rifle.

The Grand Ballroom was one room in which she spent a lot of time. The hand-carved room was constructed completely without nails. There she would play her rosewood grand piano throughout the night, or often switch back and forth between the piano and a huge organ on the opposite side of the room. Her belief was that she was providing entertainment for spirits who might wish to dance. But she suffered from severe arthritis, and it was said by those who heard her that in her later years someone else had to be playing through her fingers.

To her, another important part of the mansion was her dining hall—which was reserved exclusively for dining with the dead. The room is among the most unusual of any rooms to be found in any dwelling in the world. Large bird's-eye maple paneling, Tiffany stained-glass windows, and gold and silver leaf decorate the walls, on two of which is engraved a Shakespearean quote:

> Wide unclasp the tables of their thoughts . . .
> These same thoughts people this little world.

Sarah Winchester would sit at the head of the table in this eerie room, dressed elegantly, while twelve other places were set so that the spirits might dine with her. Each setting included a gold plate upon which was served caviar and pheasant under glass, among other gourmet foods prepared in six different kitchens by chefs from Paris and Vienna. They served her nightly in this manner, while she dined and conversed alone with her phantoms.

But it was Mrs. Winchester alone who was allowed access to the wine cellar, from which she selected each evening's offering. It was during a visit to the cellar one evening that she concluded she was to drink no more.

Upon reaching the cellar, she discovered a black handprint on the door. In horror she left the cellar and ordered it walled in and abandoned. It remains in that condition today, lost somewhere in the vast underground labyrinth of forgotten chambers and passageways.

One other time—during the 1906 earthquake—Sarah Winchester believed the spirits had finally exacted their revenge. After the tremor, she was lost for nearly an hour before servants discovered her trapped within a room where the wall had shifted into the door. She ordered the front thirty rooms sealed off and never used again, including the Grand Ballroom.

The stories of what went on within the mansion are strange, but equally interesting is how she treated those around her. It was said by many of her servants and workers that she was thoughtful and courteous, mindful of their needs. Though she was eccentric, she was a good employer. Still, her neighbors and their servants spread gossip that perhaps contributed to the reclusive manner in which Sarah Winchester lived.

On the rare occasions when she was seen in public, Mrs. Winchester would be heavily veiled. She never left her carriage or—in later years—either one of her two large Pierce-

Arrow cars, which were painted lavender and gold. Shop-keepers brought their merchandise to her, and she either accepted or rejected it on the spot.

There are those who are certain that Sarah Winchester did indeed converse with spirits throughout her life at the mansion, and that even after her natural death in 1922, those spirits remain—as well as the spirit of Sarah Winchester herself.

While Mrs. Winchester was still alive, the Blue Séance Room was another of the rooms reserved for her talks with the dead. It was here that the famous magician Houdini made one of the first visits to try to communicate with Sarah Winchester after her death. Records do not show whether or not he was successful. But the recollections of one woman who visited the Winchester Mansion indicate clearly that something unseen but powerful exists within the mansion.

Jeanne Borgan, a psychic who lives in Northern California, was involved with a number of people in a midnight séance on Halloween of 1975. Included in the group was a medium from the San Jose area and numerous members of the local press. They gathered together in the bedroom in which Sarah Winchester died. That night is one that Jeanne Borgan, as well as the others present, will not soon forget.

"I knew there were spirits in that house," Borgan recalls. "A few days before the séance I told the press that I had seen a white face and form against the wall in one of the hallways. I guess I wasn't prepared for what was to happen that Halloween night."

While they were in the death room, the air became cold and clammy. Then everyone began to visibly age.

"We all saw one man with a gray mustache who definitely didn't have any hair on his face at all," she remembers.

But it was Borgan herself who experienced the strongest and by far the strangest manifestations. Besides the gray hair, like the others, she began to develop deep lines in her face and forehead. She slumped to the floor, unable to walk or even move. There were those in the room who were sure she was having a heart attack. They took her outside, where she recovered within a few minutes, remembering nothing of the incident.

"The other people who were there with me saw it all," she says. "I didn't remember anything, just the sudden buildup of energy within myself and then feeling some kind of strange takeover. Mrs. Winchester was a powerful person."

On another occasion, psychic Sylvia Brown, co-founder of the Nirvana Foundation, spent a night with four other people inside the Winchester Mansion. They began in the séance room, where, using a tape recorder, Brown recorded organ music that she could hear; no one else heard the music, however. As they walked through the house, the group saw lights for which there were no sources and felt numerous cold spots. In the death bedroom, Brown and a writer named Antoinette May witnessed exploding balls of red light.

A woman named Arlene is said to have had a terrifying experience while visiting the mansion in 1955. While walking through one of the rooms, she mysteriously lost her eyesight. Her husband tried desperately to get her out, but they couldn't find an exit. It seems they were in the heart of the mansion. Finally they located a tour guide who escorted them outside, where the woman fully regained her eyesight.

Though no one else has had experiences within the mansion quite like those of Arlene or Jeanne Borgan or Sylvia Brown, there are a great many who have seen and heard any number of things. Tour guides, supervisors, and other mansion employees who spend a lot of time there have witnessed many unexplained things over the years. They have heard footsteps and banging doors. Windows have been slammed so hard they shatter. There have been any number of mysterious moving lights and cold spots throughout the mansion. Occasionally screws will fall from light fixtures, and doorknobs on locked doors will turn partway and then stop.

On numerous occasions an employee will hear the sound of a possible intruder and turn on a burglar alarm, only to have it not work. Lights come on after they have been shut off and doors stand unlocked after they have been secured. It is also not uncommon to hear piano and organ music, often at the same time, though the keys on the piano are broken.

It seems the different kitchen areas have seen a good share of the phantom activity over the years, including a strange morning when an office manager named Sue was taking a tour group through the mansion. Sue led the group through one of the kitchens. Sitting at the table in the kitchen was a small lady in a long dress and bonnet, who nodded to the group. Sue and the others nodded back and smiled.

"Who's the lady you hired to look like Sarah Winchester?" Sue asked her supervisor after the tour. "Who's that in the small kitchen back there?"

"What lady?" the supervisor wanted to know. "We haven't hired anybody to look like Sarah Winchester."

Upon investigating, Sue and her supervisor discovered just an empty chair moved out from the table.

On another occasion, an employee named Amy was sweeping the front kitchen when she smelled chicken soup. The odor grew quite strong, though there was no soup boiling at the time. Amy thought it might be coming from a nearby apartment building, but later realized there were no buildings near enough to have sent an odor so strong into the front kitchen.

Nearly six months later a tour guide named Gina was leading a group through the front kitchen. They all smelled chicken soup. Gina even felt a vaporous warmth, as if steam were rising from a nearby pot. Gina told the group the odor was coming from the restaurant in the gift shop, but later realized they didn't sell soup at all during the summer months.

Today the Winchester Mansion remains open to interested visitors who will likely never see a more unusual piece of construction. Nor will they ever see a monument to a more bizarre form of mental imagery than that experienced by Sarah Winchester in her attempts to escape death at the hands of unhappy spirits.

6

The Hot Springs Phantom

Chico Hot Springs Resort
Pray, Montana

The Chico Hot Springs Resort hosts many guests over the course of a year. People from around the world have come to know the stately lodge nestled against the mountains in Montana's Paradise Valley, a place for some fine cuisine and relaxation with an unbeatable view. The folks from Hollywood know Chico, as do any number of writers, adventurers, and sightseers looking for a western flavor. They all admire the lodge's turn-of-the-century architecture. But few are aware of the permanent resident on the third floor.

Tim Barnes, now the manager of security at Chico, was a skeptic about the supernatural. Housekeepers who reported strange noises and closing doors to him were met with a grin. He gave little credence to reports that footsteps could be heard when no one was around, or that kitchen plates and silverware had been left in disarray at various times.

But Tim Barnes was made a believer in the wee hours of a May morning in 1986.

A young man in his mid-twenties, Tim had been at Chico some eight years. A lot of things happen that need to be looked into by the night watchman, but the slim security guard was not prepared for what he witnessed in the darkness of the lodge that cool night.

The crowd was finally leaving the adjoining Chico Saloon. It had been another raucous Saturday night, with plenty of foot-stomping music and an occasional disagreement between patrons. But all that was over for another week and the employees in the bar were leaving for home. Barnes and another officer on duty, Ron Woolery, had just finished locking the doors. Drawing their coats around them against the chilly spring air, the two guards took the board walkway from the saloon to the main lodge.

The moon slipped behind the clouds, and the breeze rustled the pines above the parking lot. Nothing seemed out of the ordinary. In the cool silence, steam vapors rose from the hot springs pool adjacent to the saloon.

Barnes and Woolery reached the lodge, discussing the activity in the saloon. Barnes opened the door. The lobby was still, lit by three dim lamps in the ceiling. Just inside the door, Barnes stopped suddenly and Woolery bumped into him.

"What's wrong?" Woolery asked.

"Look," Barnes said, pointing across the lobby to where an old piano stood.

There, in a blurry and smoky haze, a figure hovered just above the floor near the piano. It appeared white and filmy and contained only a face and upper body, which stared at them. The rest of the figure tailed down into nothing.

Woolery gasped and Barnes stood frozen. The figure didn't move, but appeared transfixed beside the old piano, as it continued to watch the two of them. Its gaseous presence was obvious and unmistakable in the dark recesses of the quiet lobby.

The two men stared for nearly half a minute while the figure remained there, swarming in haze like thin smoke. Woolery finally managed to ask Barnes what they were seeing.

"It's obviously a ghost," Barnes said. "I guess what they've been saying about the third floor is true."

"What are we going to do?" Woolery asked.

Barnes got the idea to photograph the phantom before it vanished. That meant working his way around the check-in desk and into the office. There was a camera on one of the desks; he remembered seeing it there earlier. But walking toward a ghost was something Tim Barnes had never imagined he would ever have to do.

Deciding he needed to get a picture to prove what he and Woolery were seeing, Barnes slowly made his way toward the hovering figure. He edged around the end of the lobby desk and through the office door.

There he fumbled for a time with the Polaroid camera. He finally found a flash bar, but his trembling hands would not allow him to fit it onto the camera. Unfamiliar with the camera anyway, he decided to just take a photo and hope for the best.

Upon coming back out of the office, Barnes found the figure still hovering beside the piano. He brought the camera up and took a picture. Then the vision was gone.

"God, I can't believe what we just saw," Woolery said.

"Believe it," Barnes said. "It was there."

Inside the office, they waited for the picture to develop. Barnes commented that he wished he had had the flash bar attached, that the room was too dark for a good picture. They both commented that the owner, Mike Art, was going to be in for a shock when he read the security report.

"I wonder what he was doing down here, who he was," Woolery thought out loud.

" 'He'?" Barnes said. "I thought it was a 'she.' It seemed like a woman to me."

They studied the picture. There were no clear images. The square was black, except for three hazy spots in a row where the ceiling lamps hung, and one small white spot in the center of the picture.

"Is that tiny white spot the ghost?" Woolery wondered.

Barnes shrugged. "I doubt we'll ever know."

Ron Woolery wrote the security report that night. It read in part:

> 0200 Bar Closed, #10 off Duty.
> 0223 #10 and I Both Saw Ghost in the lobby. Tim Grabbed Camera that was in the office and tried to take a picture of it. (Picture included with Report) Ghost—dispersed. All secure.
> 0300 All secure.

The experience of Tim Barnes and Ron Woolery is by no means the first encounter with the phantom at Chico Hot Springs. Though the two security guards have so far been the only people to see the ghost for any length of time, there was one report of a New Year's Eve occurrence.

When a group of teenagers and young adults began diving into the hot springs pool from one of the roofs, a mysterious white light appeared and began moving along the eaves of the building. Some speculate that the light was trying to make the partyers get down from the roof.

The ghost—whether a "he" or a "she" or, as Tim Barnes suggests, possibly some combination—is a common manifestation that exerts a feeling of presence, most notably during the winter and early spring months. But no one can predict anything about the phantom.

The speculation as to whom the ghost or ghosts could be—or the combination of people it might be—has effectively been narrowed down to the first owners of the resort. A Pennsylvanian named William E. Knowles came to Emigrant Gulch in 1880 in search of gold. He was big and congenial and loved the outdoors. He made a lot of friends in a short time.

In 1888 he met a young woman from Ontario named Percie Matheson. She wore her long brown hair in a twist atop her head and was never one to hold back her words. She had strong opinions about drink and gambling, maintaining her refinements against all comers.

In 1891 Percie Matheson married Bill Knowles. They shared a vision of what the impressive hot springs could be if made into a resort. In the late 1890s, Bill and Percie built a boarding house near the hot springs where miners and trappers could get room and board for six dollars a week, including fresh strawberries at every meal. The warm springs nearby provided a relaxing atmosphere after a hard day of panning for gold. With business so grand, the Knowleses invested in the construction of the first hotel. On June 20, 1900, it opened for business.

The resort flourished. Guests raved about the accommodations and the adjoining bathhouses in the natural warm springs. Bill Knowles soon opened a saloon and dance hall, despite the disapproval of his wife, who spoke out adamantly against liquor and wanted it nowhere near the hotel. The fame of Chico Hot Springs grew, and the resort never lacked for patrons.

Cirrhosis of the liver killed Bill Knowles in 1910, and Percie was left in charge of the resort. She and her son, Radbourne, then twelve and the only child of the marriage, carried on with the business and made radical changes. Percie wanted no more liquor and closed the saloon. Chico began to take on a new image: it became a care center rather than a pleasure resort.

Percie Knowles secured the services of Dr. George A. Townsend and turned the resort into a hospital and sanitarium. Townsend became widely noted for his brain surgery, but he didn't stay. Other rapid changes put a twist into Knowles's plans: Radbourne soon left with a girl he wanted to marry, and paying patients became fewer and fewer. Without her son to help her manage the establishment, Knowles strained under the pressures of a resort-turned-hospital that was losing business rapidly.

Knowles, who was revered by her staff of girls, finally broke under that strain and, while confined to one of the third-floor rooms, gradually lost her mind. She was removed to a state hospital where she later died.

It seems obvious to those who have witnessed certain events that at least part of Percie Knowles is back. There is one particular rocker that seems always to end up turned so that it faces the window and Emigrant Peak, just behind the resort. It doesn't matter which room the rocker is placed in—the chair moves.

There is an attic, dusty and seldom visited and filled with old and discarded objects, where a Bible rests open on a wooden bench. The Bible is always open, yet its pages remain dust-free.

Though no one goes into the attic much anymore, there is certainly activity on the third floor, where there are a number of old rooms, including number 49, in which Percie Knowles was confined during her lengthy illness. One other room, believed to be a favorite of Bill Knowles before he died, also contains an unexplained feeling.

The majority of the stories circulate among the workers.

Each has his or her idea as to the ghost's gender. Some are sure it is female; others, while speaking unconsciously, often refer to the manifestation as "he."

Various housekeepers have reported that they felt a presence in the room while changing sheets on a bed. As one housekeeper explains it, "I just feel he is there. I hum to myself and hurry up and get my work done and get out of there. Sometimes I even ask him to please leave until I'm done. I don't like the feeling."

Another caretaker will no longer work on the third-floor, not after she heard a door slam when she was the only one on that level at the time.

Others also have heard doors slamming and footsteps along the third floor hallway. It is not uncommon for the kitchen help to find the silverware and plates in disarray when they come in to get the dining room ready for breakfast guests.

One of the women working at the check-in desk reported that during the spring of 1987, a woman from Billings, Montana, who said she had psychic powers, felt the presence of a female phantom on the third floor.

"She seemed to be content," the woman told the desk clerk. "But there is definitely someone up there."

Are the old owners still in residence? Is there a reason why Chico maintains its Old West style and feeling? As can be said about some places, Chico has its own personality. Bill and Percie Knowles seem to be that personality.

The resort has had various owners since the Knowleses's time. Most recently, under the innovative management of Mike Art, the complex has evolved into a haven for those who want something different and rustic. It has become widely known through word-of-mouth and through travel magazine writers. The little resort at Chico provides welcome hospitality to a lot of people who wish to see part of the Old West in a valley crowded by the twentieth century.

The mysterious noises and the sound of footsteps on the third floor are also becoming widely known. Perhaps Bill and Percie Knowles may still be there, residing in this quaint little retreat they both loved so dearly.

7

The Lost
Trail Hotel

The Lost Trail Hotel
Southwestern Arizona

Sunday newspapers often publish interesting feature articles, some of which can lead to life-changing experiences. Though certainly not all Sunday supplements are aimed at altering the way in which we live, some articles have been known to alter the way we look at death.

George Gardiner of Sonoita, Arizona, is a case in point. A tall and mild-mannered man of middle age, Gardiner cannot pass up an interesting place to go and look around. In constant search for interesting sites to explore with his wife, Wilma, he will adjust his glasses and take in all the details when he hears or reads something about the past.

Gardiner's experience with the odd forms of life after death occurred on a spring night in 1976. It all began with an article he read in the *Tucson Daily Star* about an old hotel at the edge of a little town nestled in the lonely desert country not far from the Mexico and New Mexico borders.

The small and unique Lost Trail Hotel had a lot to offer guests who wanted the flavor of the Old West. Mrs. Croft, the manager, had been there thirty years and was known for her smile and hospitality. Steak or chicken was served nightly. You could have one or the other, but not both. The hotel had only five rooms, so it was essential to call ahead for reservations.

"Nothing has changed but a few light fixtures," George told Wilma as he read the article.

Wilma was as interested as her husband. The couple quickly sold themselves on the idea of driving into the desert to find the Lost Trail Hotel.

Retired from a successful real estate business, George spends his time traveling with Wilma and writing articles and books about the West, both contemporary and historical. He also makes medicine pipes for the Western Writers of America, pipes that are presented yearly as the Medicine Pipe Bearer's Award to the writer of the best first Western novel of the year.

The pipe is an original each year and is a work of fine craftsmanship. Those who are lucky enough to receive the Medicine Pipe Bearer's Award in the form of one of George Gardiner's pieces of art cherish it throughout their lives.

With the Lost Trail Hotel and its unique story grabbing his imagination, George finished reading the article. He learned that there was an old Wells Fargo freight office there, and a railroad track ran along the outskirts of town, an old track abandoned for more than fifty years. Here was a town and an adobe hotel as old as the West itself, with nothing changed.

It was midweek when George and Wilma packed up for the overnight stay at the Lost Trail Hotel. They had called ahead for reservations and had reached the elderly Mrs. Croft. In her crackly but mannerly voice she assured them of a room and a good meal. She told them how to get there, and how to avoid the worst roads—the roads that led into the desert.

From their Sonoita home, George and Wilma departed on what they concluded would be a full afternoon's drive into the historic region where Chiricahua Apaches made their last desperate stand against the bluecoat soldiers sent to track them down. The U.S. Army proved relentless and too numerous for the Apache. Before that last gasp of freedom, the Apache nation had been a strong people. They had warred for many years against the spreading Spanish settlements, and in earlier days against the powerful Comanche. Now this history was but dust and xeric vegetation that harbored a little known remnant of the past. Of the years of dreams and culture, all that was left was a monument.

George and Wilma drove through the desert toward Lost Trail and its historic hotel. It would be a direct link with history, a little adobe building that had been built a century earlier, that few tourists knew existed.

The Gardiners grew restless to get there. But on this spring day, with the desert popping into full bloom around them, George Gardiner had no way of knowing that nightfall in the Lost Trail Hotel would bring him a vision he would never be able to explain.

George and Wilma arrived at Lost Trail in the early evening. It was every bit what they had expected. You couldn't even call it a town, just a collection of a few adobe huts and a few clapboard buildings nestled alongside a small stream. On the other side of the stream, as history recounts, was deadly country. Apaches had made a last stand in the desert and raided the town from their position. Lost Trail had seen its share of bloody streets.

Near the edge of the little town was an adobe structure a little larger than the others, with a creaky wooden sign hanging over the door. Scrawled in badly faded Old English lettering were the words: *Lost Trail Hotel.*

A small lady in a blue shawl met them at the door with a smile. Mrs. Croft. Her soft blue eyes were wrapped with wrinkles and tanned skin. She tilted her head in greeting, her long coils of snow-white hair wrapped in a bun and tied up with gemstone pins and a net. She blinked her blue eyes as she spoke.

"Welcome, folks. I'm Mrs. Croft. Come inside."

George and Wilma stepped into a parlor of antique furnishings that included a hand-carved Palo Verde wood sofa upholstered in blue velvet and a rocking chair. While they registered, they noticed several other old chairs and a washstand on which a hand-painted china bowl stood with a matching china pitcher that was filled with water from a well just out back. Mrs. Croft smiled and mentioned that she had never been to Sonoita, but wanted to travel there some day.

George and Wilma noted the narrow hallway as they followed Mrs. Croft to their room. There was but one light fixture in the hallway, a carbide light that had been converted and now shone dimly with a twenty-five-watt electrical bulb. Inside the room there was a single cord fixture hanging from the ceiling near an old bed of curved and scrolled brass. A bath and washbasin had been built into one corner of the room.

Mrs. Croft smiled and said, "Your meal will be ready in just a few minutes," then ambled out of the room.

George and Wilma changed into fresh clothes and upon reentering the parlor found Mrs. Croft arranging antique dinnerware and glasses on a walnut table covered with a red-checked tablecloth. She finished by placing settings of stainless-steel cutlery that had been brought out on a wagon train.

George noticed place settings for just the two of them. He asked Mrs. Croft if he and Wilma would be the only guests this evening. He received a smile and a polite nod from the old lady, busy with her place setting. She remarked that it was a little early in the year for guests on a regular basis.

Mrs. Croft went to the kitchen and returned with a plate of chicken and another of mashed potatoes. She then brought out a plate of homemade rolls and an apple pie.

"Enjoy your stay," she said. "I'll be next door if you need anything."

After the meal, George and Wilma toured the adjacent Wells Fargo office. An old safe sat along the back wall, and a record book lay on a desk, just as they had a century before. There was an old couch where patrons waited and where the locals of the time no doubt gathered to chat and hear the latest news from Tombstone, Tucson, and other parts of the state. Outside, the tracks sat rusting on long-rotted ties. Weather-beaten markers were visible in a little graveyard on a hill above the creek. In its heyday, Lost Trail had seen many diverse people. Some of them, George Gardiner would soon learn, remained behind in one form or another.

The pleasant evening passed into nightfall. George and Wilma strolled back inside the hotel, and after doing some reading, decided it was time to call it a night. After Wilma got into bed, George turned off the switch on the bare bulb hanging from the ceiling, and the room was plunged into darkness.

It had been a long day, and in a few minutes Wilma was sound asleep. George lay in the darkness with thoughts of the little town and the desert running through his head. Exploring historical places always invigorated him and got him to thinking about the past. This energy often kept him thinking long into the night. Tonight was one of those nights, and he knew he wouldn't get to sleep right away.

It was then that the strange noise began in the hall—the odd crying.

George was at once perplexed and alarmed. He felt the

hair on the back of his neck rising. He sat up in bed while the odd crying continued. It sounded like a woman weeping and wailing—a wavering sound that spoke of terrible mourning. It clearly was coming from out in the hall. Wilma continued to sleep, even though to him the sounds seemed quite loud and unnerving.

George began to wonder if he indeed was hearing the wailing, or if it was his imagination. But the wailing grew louder and closer.

Is that a woman crying out in the hall? What in the world is wrong out there?

The darkness closed in even blacker now, and George felt a clammy sensation enveloping him. He continued to sit upright in bed, almost frozen. The wailing continued, unmistakably the sound of a woman in terrible distress. George didn't know what to do about Wilma. She still had not awakened. He decided to let her sleep. The wailing seemed to be moving up the hall now, slowly, past the door.

George made himself get out of bed. *What if someone needs help?* He forced himself through the inky darkness toward the door, where the wailing was now the loudest. He took a deep breath and gripped the doorknob. It creaked and the door came back toward him.

The hallway was in heavy shadow from the poor lighting, but it took no light to see the big ball of white mist that was floating along the ceiling, moving toward one corner. In the middle of the mist was a woman's head, turned almost sideways, with eyes opened wide.

George froze against the wall next to the doorjamb, trying to comprehend what he was seeing. Numb with shock, he watched as the head suspended itself near a corner of the ceiling. The wailing continued. The woman's lips were full and bright red, her hair long and black. She stared from the ball of light, her complexion waxy and smooth, like that of a statue.

Her head was turned, as if she might be resting on a pillow. The vision made him want to yell, but his breath was caught in his throat.

Suddenly the apparition rose like evaporating mist into the ceiling, and the hallway was again black and silent. George quivered and made himself move. The only sound was a scraping against old wood as George, pressed tightly against the wall, backed through the doorway into the room.

His senses reeling with terror, George slid inside and pushed the door closed with trembling hands. His mind tried to reject what his eyes had just seen. His chest rose and fell with his breath as he fumbled across the room, reaching for the hanging light bulb. He shuffled and groped and stumbled against objects in the darkness until he finally found the suspended bulb and turned on the switch.

Wilma had never awakened and was still sleeping, her back to the light. George was mystified. His wife hadn't heard or felt anything? He put an arm on her shoulder but decided against waking her to tell her what he had just witnessed. What would she think? Would she tell him he had been dreaming? He didn't want to appear foolish. Besides, what good would it do to scare her as well? He considered turning off the light and dismissing the entire incident. But it had all seemed just as real as his wife still lying in restful sleep.

George was beginning to doubt himself now—wondering if what had happened was real, or merely a dream. But he was still shaking and could see vividly in his mind the statuelike head with the black hair and the red lips. He knew he would always see it. This was nothing like a dream.

No, it had been real. George knew that the head was not something his imagination could have created on its own. Nothing could convince him that the noise and the vision hadn't appeared. There was no question he had seen a ghost.

Then George began to feel something resembling sorrow.

Beyond the horror of the woman's image was a sense of bleak despair. It seemed to permeate the blind fear that George had felt upon first seeing the vision. What terrible thing had happened to the woman? Who was she? Had she been of Indian or Hispanic blood, with her long black hair and solemn eyes? And why was she here, in just the form of a head tilted in white mist?

George Gardiner couldn't answer any of his questions. He turned off the bare bulb and tried to sleep, but couldn't. Instead, he sat awake watching the door, listening, dreading the silence that might at any time again erupt into that woeful wailing.

But neither the wailing nor the vision returned during that night. For a long time George lay in the darkness, considering what he had seen and why. He finally decided it would probably never be explained.

The next morning, George and Wilma packed and headed back to Sonoita. They didn't see Mrs. Croft, who stayed next door in her little house. She didn't serve breakfast—just dinner. George wondered if the old lady knew anything about what existed inside the Lost Trail Hotel.

On the way home, George told Wilma about his experience and she listened without comment. That kind of thing just didn't happen. George certainly wished it hadn't happened.

Over the years the topic was discussed only at brief and infrequent intervals. The few friends George chose to discuss it with listened and nodded, understanding, but unable to explain what had happened to him. These friends were a choice few who might know what it meant, since they had had similar experiences. Some had seen things, some hadn't, but all had felt something at one time or another. His friends told him the desert held many secrets and no one would ever fully understand them.

Over the years, George Gardiner came to realize that the floating head in the Lost Trail Hotel was an experience he could neither deny nor understand. It meant only one thing for certain: the dead of the Arizona desert country are not all resting in peace.

8

The Cries of Millie Pratt

The Old Pratt Hotel
Central Colorado

Among the oldest hotels in Colorado are those atop the Rocky Mountains, built during the days of the gold and silver booms of the last century. One of those said to be among the first built is the Old Pratt Hotel, located in the middle of a small town in the mountains of central Colorado.

More significant than the Old West flavor of the hotel is the terrifying legacy that haunts its three stories—a strange series of events that began just after the Civil War and continues, some say, through the present. The present owners insist it is all hearsay and sensationalism, something created for publicity, something they want nothing to do with. They go as far as to say it is all the product of somebody's dreams. But on a late fall night in 1977, Marilyn Johnson experienced much more than a dream, and the memory returns to her whenever she sees a staircase.

Johnson, then in her late thirties, had been a practicing

registered nurse since completing college. She and her husband, Mike, resided in New Orleans and were visiting the West for the first time. Mike had a brother in Denver he hadn't seen for a number of years. Their idea was to visit Mike's brother and then see the authentic Old West, as it was preserved in the Rocky Mountains in the central and western part of Colorado.

Marilyn and Mike had been looking forward to this vacation for a number of months. Colorado's story fascinated them. History was made during the heyday of the first mining era; it would be interesting to learn about it. And during the fall, with most travelers back home, the towns wouldn't be as crowded. Marilyn hardly suspected she would encounter something from the past that she would rather not have encountered.

After visiting Mike's brother the couple traveled for the better part of a week, visiting small towns in the mountains and relaxing at campgrounds. Toward the end of the week they came to a little town at the top of a mountain pass. It was quaint, the picture of early Colorado. There were numerous small shops to browse in and a large museum that contained a trove of local and state history. There was a lot to see and do, and since it was midafternoon, it might be just the place to spend the night.

Mike suggested they stay at the Old Pratt Hotel at the edge of town. It was an old Victorian structure that boasted of being one of the first built in Colorado. There was antique but well-kept maroon carpeting in parts of the lobby, and exquisite chandeliers hung from the ceiling. The railings were hardwood, as was the stairway, and the rooms were furnished with antique dressers and china bowls and water pitchers.

Marilyn cherished the view of the mountains from the third floor, and they asked for the room closest to the stairway. They were told the room was being readied for remodeling, and would they mind the room next to it. Marilyn remarked that the room by the stairs offered the best view of the mountains. Mike offered to pay extra, and the woman at the desk called the manager.

"You really want that room?" the manager asked.

"It has a big window," Marilyn said. "I would like it for that reason, to see the mountains."

The manager thought for a moment. Finally he nodded. The Johnsons got the room they wanted, right next to the staircase.

Marilyn and Mike strolled around the town, which included a large park and an area of new houses and stores to accommodate mine workers moving in for a construction project. The older part of town seemed somewhat segregated, and it occurred to Marilyn and Mike that not many people were staying at the Old Pratt Hotel. Most everyone was at the newer motel and hotel complexes closer to the main highway.

After an evening of sightseeing and browsing the shops, Marilyn and Mike settled into their room for the night.

"I suddenly got this sad feeling," Marilyn recalls. "It wasn't anything I could explain at the time, but it was a sad feeling, like I wanted to cry."

It didn't seem that Mike was experiencing the same thing, so Marilyn just dismissed it. She hung her clothes in the small closet near the bed, while Mike laid his clothes out on an old rocker. Then Marilyn spent some time watching the sun set behind the mountains, with the odd feeling that someone small was standing beside her, watching the same sunset. Marilyn attributed the feeling to the fact that she and Mike had never been in the mountains before, or in an old hotel like this. She just wasn't accustomed to it—certainly it wasn't anything more than that.

Marilyn and Mike left the room and went to a small café a short way down the street. The Old Pratt Hotel hadn't served meals in years, though the kitchen remained intact and the dining room's tables were set with blue china plates and crystal glassware.

"We just want to keep it authentic," the manager told Mike when he asked about it. "Someday we'll reopen for dining and we want to keep the atmosphere of the place.

Later, when Marilyn and Mike returned from the café to go to bed, Marilyn became uneasy again. She looked into the closet, sure that her clothes had been rearranged, but knowing she hadn't touched them herself.

The couple went to bed, and while Mike rested comfortably beside her, Marilyn tried to understand what was bothering her. She decided she hadn't paid enough attention to how she had placed her clothes in the closet, and that she was just tired from the almost two weeks of traveling. All she needed was a good night's sleep.

Marilyn finally managed to fall asleep, though not soundly. More than once she awoke feeling uncomfortable but not knowing why. Then sometime late in the night she began to hear sounds.

"It began in the clothes closet," she remembers. "I could hear the hangers knocking together. I knew it was the hangers, that's what it sounded like. But I didn't want to believe it."

The rustling in the closet stopped, and Marilyn decided she would try again to fall asleep. But now there were noises in the hall, as if someone small were skipping on the hardwood. Then there was a knock at the door. The knocking ended and the skipping began again.

Marilyn couldn't remember anyone having a small child up on this floor, and certainly none would be up this time of night. But the sounds ended and Marilyn took another deep breath. Then began her trip into the most shocking event of her life.

"I was almost asleep when I heard the voice," Marilyn recalls. "It sounded like a little girl. She said 'Mommy?' and it seemed like it was right next to my ear."

Marilyn gasped and jumped up in bed. This awoke Mike and he turned on a lamp near the bed. Marilyn tried to tell herself she had been dreaming, while Mike stared and asked her what was the matter.

"I don't know," she managed to say. "I guess I was dreaming or something."

Mike turned out the light and Marilyn snuggled up next to him under the covers. Soon he was fast asleep again. Then the whimpering sounds began. Again, it sounded as if they were near the bed, sounds of a small child crying softly. The whimpering grew louder as Marilyn froze. Finally she heard the words "Mommy . . . Mommy."

Marilyn reached over Mike and turned on the light. She was afraid to turn around but finally did, only to see empty space next to the bed. She lay next to her sleeping husband in the silence of the room, hearing only her own breathing. Her nerves were taut and she was trying to decide what it was exactly that had happened. She thought about waking Mike again, then she heard the sounds in the hallway.

Again it was the unmistakable sound of little feet moving along the hardwood floor. The *click, a-click, a-click, a-click* of a child skipping down the hall, coming closer to their bedroom.

Marilyn held her breath as the footsteps went past their door and seemed to stop. She waited for the knock, and began to shake Mike, but stopped when once again there was no sound.

Then, near the head of the stairway, it sounded as if someone were pounding on the wall. Marilyn was certain now that someone's daughter was wandering the halls. She got out of bed and, leaving the light on in their room, went to the door and opened it.

There was one small light just past their room on the hallway wall. It gave out a dim glow that showed the bare floor. Marilyn squinted to see. She never did see anything in those shadows, but the noise she then heard made her scream and run back into the room. They were thudding, clumping sounds, as if someone were falling down the stairs.

Marilyn closed the door and started to yell. Mike woke up then and tried to get her to talk, to tell him what had happened. Marilyn said she thought she had heard someone falling down the stairs. Mike went out to look, but there was no one anywhere on the stairs.

"Maybe it was somebody running down the stairs," Mike suggested. "Maybe a prowler."

The night clerk arrived within a few minutes, along with other guests, and the story of what had happened quickly became distorted. Soon everyone was looking for a man who had started running down the stairs when Marilyn opened the door, possibly a burglar. But the outside doors were locked, and there was no sign anyone had broken through any of the windows.

Neither Mike nor Marilyn went back to sleep that night. Marilyn insisted she had heard someone on the stairs, that she hadn't been dreaming, but Mike didn't buy her story. He knew that she would awaken on occasion back home, talking about someone she was caring for at the hospital. Marilyn always seemed to get close to her patients.

It was years later that Marilyn finally told Mike the full story of what had happened that night in Colorado at the Old Pratt Hotel. She told him because she knew he would believe her. And he did, because he had just had a paranormal experience of his own—the appearance of an old man on a fishing vessel he had been working on, when there were only two younger men with him on board at the time.

Marilyn Johnson's terrifying night at the Old Pratt Hotel is one of many unexplained occurrences that have happened over the years. Stories of a mysterious little girl abound, and they cannot be denied.

Often guests will appear at the check-in counter and report a little girl on one of the floors who had just approached them to ask if they have seen her mommy. If the attendant at the desk has worked there very long, he or she will shrug and say they will check on it.

On one occasion a woman in tears was helped down the stairs by her husband. She reported having seen a small girl lying at the foot of the third-floor stairway, who then vanished before her eyes.

It is all connected to the history of the Old Pratt Hotel. It is one of the first to be built in Colorado, having been constructed by William Ludley Pratt, who, fresh from the Union Army, made his fortune in gold during the late 1860s. Pratt and his wife had one child, a girl named Millie.

It is said that little Millie lost her mother to tuberculosis when Millie was just five. Her father, busy with running the hotel as well as his interests in mining, left Millie in the care of an older woman who stayed with her on the third floor. But the old woman was crippled and spent a lot of time in a rocking chair. Millie was left to fend for herself most of the time.

Millie, as the legend goes, never got over the loss of her mother. She believed that her mother was there, that she had seen her, and she would look for her all the time. Then came a late afternoon when the hallways were dark with shadows and somehow Millie fell down the stairs to her death.

Soon after, William Ludley Pratt sold his mining interests and the hotel that bears his name. He had the bodies of his wife and daughter shipped to the East and reinterred there. When Pratt himself died early in the 1900s he was given full military honors and buried with his family. Though Millie's body may have been taken from the Colorado mountaintop, her spirit remained in the hotel.

A former employee, a head housekeeper named Ellen, said she had several encounters with Millie, including one on the Fourth of July in 1972.

"I saw her in a room on the first floor at the back of the hotel," Ellen remembers. "I thought it was one of the guests who had dressed up in old-time clothes for the parade. She looked like a little girl from the 1800s with her hair made up in ringlets. She smiled at me and I smiled back."

When Ellen remarked to one of the maids working under her that she had seen the little girl, the maid looked at her strangely and said she had just seen a little girl fitting that description not five minutes before on the third floor.

"It was Millie Pratt," Ellen said later. "A family portrait of the Pratts was on a wall in the dining room. This little girl was sitting on her mother's lap—the same little girl. She had the same little hat and her hair was in ringlets."

Others among the maids who have worked at the Old Pratt Hotel remember a cold spot that used to follow them around the building when they worked. Though a couple of the maids quit after that, the others stayed on and paid it no mind, commenting that it was just Millie following the help around like she used to do when she was alive, more than a hundred years ago.

Seeing Millie has happened to but a few; hearing her has happened to many. The skipping in the hall and the pounding on the doors and walls seems to be a common manifestation. It is said that, if only for a second or two, the smell of flower-scented perfume will sometimes fill the hall, as well as the room where she was confined as a child.

The thumping on the stairs has been heard by a few others as well; and a woman claiming to be a psychic checked in and out within an hour, saying that a little girl had met her death here and that the energy left behind was too strong for her to bear. She got her money back and never returned.

Though Millie Pratt makes her phantom presence known most often, there are other manifestations in the Old Pratt Hotel. One story tells of a woman staying alone who checked out after opening the door of her room to see a man standing next to her dresser, wearing what she thought was an old cavalry uniform. Others have seen the man as well, including a historian who saw him at the foot of his bed at dawn one morning. They are all convinced he is the ghost of Millie's father in his Civil War uniform.

"I never did see the soldier," Ellen says. "I know a couple of the maids saw him, and then just fleetingly, like he was there a split second and then gone. But they remembered the blue of his dress, like a uniform."

Some wonder whether or not Millie's father may have returned dressed as he had been the first day he saw Colorado. It is thought that perhaps William Ludley Pratt is hoping, even in death, that he can make things right for his lost little daughter.

The Old Pratt Hotel will be in the mountains of central Colorado for years to come, and will continue to cater to guests who wish to partake of the past. Those who don't believe that phantoms roam there will be happy with those thoughts and live contentedly.

But there will be those who won't agree. Some will always wonder if a man in a Civil War uniform isn't trying to start his earthly life over at the hotel, even though he has been dead for nearly a century. Possibly he wants to give his daughter another chance to live out her own earthly life. But it is too late, and the spirit of Millie Pratt may still wander the halls and stairways of her father's hotel, looking for her mother.

9

The Ghost in
the Sheridan Inn

Sheridan Inn
Sheridan, Wyoming

Sunday morning sunlight broke through the window of
George Carmichael's room on the third floor of the Sheridan
Inn. Carmichael was a musician who had played the piano in
the dining room each evening since the preceding fall. Me-
mentos of times past were everywhere, including pictures of
Buffalo Bill Cody and members of his Wild West Show from
early in the century.

Despite its reputation for a rowdy past, the inn was a quiet
place where people came to relax and enjoy a good meal. It
was widely known for its heritage and its personality, and the
community had come to cherish the old hotel. Nothing about
the place had ever bothered George Carmichael, until that
bright Sunday morning in May 1970.

He awoke in his bed and blinked a couple of times. Something didn't seem right to him. He turned to one of the windows facing the mountains and saw a woman standing there,

gazing out into the morning. She was wearing a long, light-blue dress.

"Can I help you?" Carmichael asked. "Is there something you want?"

He had been searching for words. He could not understand why a woman in an old blue dress would be standing in his room looking out the window. Furthermore, he couldn't understand how she got into his room. He always kept the door locked at night.

The woman seemed to be ignoring him, so he asked her again politely what he could do for her. She then turned to him and, in an instant, dissolved before his eyes.

His breath caught in his throat. For a time he couldn't move; he just stared at the window where the woman had been. When he was finally able to get out of bed, he quickly put on a bathrobe and rushed downstairs.

He was met by the kitchen help, who for a moment couldn't understand what he was saying. Carmichael was always quiet and well mannered. He kept to himself and out of people's way. He wasn't a drinker, and in fact stayed away from it for the most part. This was the first time most of them had ever heard him say more than a few words at a time. Something unusual had just happened to George Carmichael.

Aware of how he appeared, standing white-faced in his bathrobe, Carmichael finally told the gathering of kitchen and dining room help that he had seen a woman upstairs, a woman who had vanished before his eyes.

Surprisingly enough, no one seemed to question him in the least. No one even seemed to think his story too unusual. One of the help then remarked, "You've seen Miss Kate. She still lives up there."

"Miss Kate Arnold," one of the other women said matter-of-factly. "They say she's still here, watching over the inn."

No one had told George Carmichael about this and he

The Blue Light Lady
The statue of Elizabeth Poly in a public park named in her honor. She looks across the town of Hays, Kansas, toward her final resting place on Sentinel Hill. (Robert Wilhelm)

The Legacy of Winchester Mansion
The elaborate features of Sarah Winchester's Victorian mansion provide a
picturesque background for this restored fountain at the Winchester
Mystery House in San Jose, California. (Winchester Mystery House)

The Legacy of Winchester Mansion
San Jose's lady of mystery, Sarah Winchester—
heiress to the Winchester Rifle fortune. Mrs.
Sarah L. Winchester was mistress and occultly
inspired architect of Winchester Mystery
House from 1884–1922. Her five-and-a-half
million-dollar mansion has been called "a
monument to a woman's fears." It is open
daily, except Christmas, from 9:00 A.M. and
attracts visitors from all over the world. The
160-room structure is located on Winchester
Blvd. and I-280, near the intersection of state
highway #17. Likeness is close-up photo of
figure of Mrs. Winchester in the Winchester
Historical Museum, adjacent to Winchester
Mystery House. (Winchester Mystery House)

Visions of Reno Crossing
Second Lieutenant Benjamin H. Hodgson, killed at Reno Crossing. His spirit
still haunts the battlefield. (Little Bighorn Battlefield National Monument)

Visions of Reno Crossing
The mysterious stone house on the Little Bighorn Battlefield, located adjacent to the cemetery, where many unusual things have happened, has been renovated for use as the new library. (author photo)

The Hot Springs Phantom
Percie Knowles, who once owned the Chico Hot Springs Resort, still haunts the inn and the area around the hot pools. (Bill and Doris Whithorn Collection)

The Phantoms of Fort Laramie
The cavalry barracks at Fort Laramie National Historic Site, where it is said the boots of cavalry soldiers can be heard at dawn, thundering along the boardwalk, answering the call to reveille. (author photo)

The Ghost in the Sheridan Inn
The Sheridan Inn, often called the House of 69 Gables, where the ghost of Miss Kate Arnold still roams. (author photo)

The Ghost in the Sheridan Inn
The room where Miss Kate lived in the Sheridan Inn. Her ashes were placed in the wall behind the nightstand. (author photo)

The Mystery of the Little People
The mummified remains of a small humanoid
being, found in the Pedro Mountains near Casper,
Wyoming, in the summer of 1932. Many believe this
is proof of the Little People, a race of mysterious
and sacred beings from American Indian lore.
(Wyoming Division of Cultural Resources)

promptly quit his job at the piano in the dining room. He realized he would never be able to get a night's sleep in the inn again.

Though George was frightened by what he saw, many others who know of her presence in the inn say there is nothing to fear from Miss Kate, unless you make her mad. The tiny spinster who was a scullery maid, a seamstress, and a housekeeper at the inn, spent sixty-five years of her life there. She came to call it her own, at least within her own mind. And everyone who knew her acknowledged that Miss Kate loved the inn more than anyone else ever could have.

Some say she still loves that inn better than any other place she might ever have visited—even in death.

Kate Arnold came to Sheridan, Wyoming, as a young woman of twenty-one. She got off a train and looked across a wagon-rutted street to where the inn stood. It had been built as a joint venture by the Sheridan Land Company and the Burlington and Missouri Railroad, and had opened in 1893. By now, in July of 1901, it was flourishing.

The inn was owned by Buffalo Bill Cody for a number of years. Miss Kate saw to it that Cody and his many guests were comfortable and well cared for. Some say her spirit longs for those days to return, and she wanders the old hotel waiting for Cody to bring back the good times.

Miss Kate saw the good times decline as the twentieth century exerted its influence over America. With cars and planes and boats, people wanted to see the rest of the world. The Sheridan Inn declined, though Miss Kate did anything she could to see that the historic landmark received its due respect. During the years of the inn's worst decline, Miss Kate was often one of the few who lived there. She could be seen on her hands and knees, working to mend the deteriorating carpets by hand.

Then Miss Kate's health started to fail, seemingly like the

inn, and she began to despair. New hope for the inn eventually arrived with a new owner, a woman now known as just Neltje. Under Neltje's supervision, remodeling began and the inn took on new life. Miss Kate, who was promised a room when the work was completed, moved out to a place where she could be cared for until her room was ready. She never got to live in that room during her flesh-and-blood existence, for soon after moving she died.

But Neltje kept her promise to Miss Kate. She kept the room on the third floor for her and her alone, never renting it to anyone. Miss Kate's ashes were placed in one of the walls and her belongings were returned to the room. Against the wall was placed a small nightstand with a pink silk flower, which remained there in memoriam to the little woman who so dearly loved the inn.

When the inn was reopened, the intent was to attract the younger generation. The inn needed to show a profit if it was to survive. Besides the dining room, the old saloon was remodeled, and the Buffalo Bill Bar opened up, complete with entertainment for the younger set.

Rumors began to circulate among the help that Miss Kate was upset with the new arrangements. Rock musicians who played the Buffalo Bill Bar complained frequently about their instruments going out of tune for no apparent reason, or unusual sounds coming from their amplifiers. One musician insisted his guitar fell from its stand on its own, cracking the neck.

A manager who worked in a shop in the lobby for eleven years claimed to have the explanation for the musicians' troubles. "Miss Kate doesn't like rock music," she said. "She couldn't stand it."

The former manager recalled that one evening while a band performed, she saw a bottle crash into one of the walls at the rear of the bar. It was early in the evening and there were few patrons. The music was loud enough, the manager said, so that hardly anyone heard the bottle crash. But she did. And she knew it couldn't have been thrown by anyone near the wall, for they were all drinking their beer from cans.

The kitchen help often had to rearrange place settings mysteriously scattered on the dining-room tables. Often the plates and silverware that had been put out by the evening help for breakfast would disappear from the tables by morning. Those on the first shift would find the plates and utensils neatly put away in the kitchen.

Monna Monk, a resident of Sheridan, Wyoming, was a bookkeeper at the Sheridan Inn for a number of years. She listened to the stories with skepticism and often told the women that they had vivid imaginations.

"I really didn't believe all that," Monk says. "Then one morning Miss Kate made a believer out of me."

Monk and some of the others who worked at the inn were having coffee. Monk had just checked out the two old cash registers that were used to ring up sales. The old registers had several drawers and a lever that was pulled down to total the entries.

"We were sitting there discussing Miss Kate's ghost," Monk recalls. "I laughed and told one of the gals that their stories were getting pretty comical. Suddenly those two cash registers started ringing up by themselves. The levers came down and the drawers flew out and we all sat there staring. Later I told Miss Kate I believed she was there and that I would appreciate it if she wouldn't bother me. She didn't."

Even more extraordinary is the story of a long-time caretaker named Bruno, who has since died. As caretaker of the grounds, Bruno lived in a room on the second floor. When the inn closed and Bruno moved out, he told many people of his repeated encounters with Miss Kate's spirit. She would often visit him during the night and sit on the edge of his bed. Though he was able to see through her, she weighed down the mattress.

Their discussions were mental. She was worried about what was going to happen to the old hotel, because everything was changing so fast and people no longer seemed to care about the old days and what life was like then. Bruno listened to her many times. When she was finished, she would get up from the bed and drift into the blackness of the hallway.

Everyone who ever had an encounter with the ghost of Miss Kate seemed aware that she was disturbed about the changes that were occurring, that the West was becoming a different place. Doors slammed and lights blew out for reasons no one could understand. Curtains were changed around and furniture moved, all because Miss Kate wanted the Old West to remain within the Sheridan Inn.

Neltje, who did her best to compromise between the demands of the patrons and the wishes of Miss Kate was acutely aware of the ghostly maid's change in mood. She would often go to Miss Kate's room, where the ashes of the former housekeeper were buried in the wall, and try to make amends for things that had happened. The silk flower on the nightstand was always an indicator of how Miss Kate's spirit felt that day.

"I always tried to keep Miss Kate happy with the way things were going," Neltje says. "But she would become angry at times and knock the silk flower off the nightstand. I don't know how many times I put it back up there."

Finally, the stress of inadequate finances and the hardships of keeping competent help grew to be such a strain on Neltje that she could see no alternative but to close the inn. It changed hands and after a brief time, closed once again.

Today the Sheridan Inn has been reopened, and is under management by the Sheridan Heritage Center. The room reserved for Miss Kate still contains her suitcase and an old rocker, both covered with dust. And on the small nightstand against the wall where Kate's ashes lie, still rests the pink silk flower—clean and completely dust free.

In the Sheridan Inn, where the Old West lives in phantom form, there still exists a feeling of majesty and grandeur. Incredible emotion lingers from the past, and permeates those who visit even today. The mounted buffalo head over the fireplace and the scores of historic photos that line the wall all look out with a life that comes from within each of them.

Some say the spirit of Miss Kate is as restless as ever wandering the halls, overseeing events. It is said that the drapery in the ballroom will sometimes move, as if someone is looking out. Miss Kate always loved the ballroom, for it was the scene of many happy times.

Miss Kate came to love the inn as she would a child, something to nurture and see grow strong and healthy. She has to be happy that the inn has reopened. Perhaps her spirit will never pass from the site.

10

The Gambler

St. James Hotel
Cimarron, New Mexico

In May of 1993, Greg Champion journeyed to New Mexico from Dana Point, California, to visit the St. James Hotel. His intention was to tour the hotel and perhaps buy the property. Little did Greg know that he was stepping into the historic past, which was still very much alive.

"I had heard that the hotel was haunted," Greg said later, "but I had never put much credence in that sort of thing. I'm a skeptic. But there are a lot of things that have gone on here that I can't explain."

Greg was touring the hotel with Ed Sitzberger, one of the previous owners, videotaping each room as he went. The historical aspects were many and could easily be used in promotional material.

Greg's last stop was the notorious Room 18, where no guests are allowed to stay. One of the tenants, it is said, has never left the room, a tenant who exhibits anger toward intruders.

Some time in the 1880s, the room had been rented to a gambler named T. J. Wright, who had been gunned down in a dispute over a card game. The stakes were said to be the hotel itself. T. J. Wright had won the hand, but had paid his life in the settlement of the debt.

It is said that his spirit still haunts the room and is difficult to deal with. The previous owners kept the door locked at all times, prohibiting any guests from staying there.

"As I was videotaping the entire hotel, I told Mr. Sitzberger that I had to see the room," Greg recalls. "He warned me that strange things could happen."

"I taped the room, seeing a card table and a bar with a bottle of Jack Daniel's and shot glasses. Nothing seemed out of the ordinary. Mr. Sitzberger was surprised that nothing went wrong. It was when I got back to California that I realized there was really something going on in the St. James Hotel."

As manager of a hotel in Dana Point, Greg had always wanted his own place, to handle in the manner he saw fit. He had liked the St. James very much. No one had known of his trip to Cimarron. Upon his return, though, a woman named Jennifer, who worked in reservations, gave him the shock of his life.

"I didn't know Jennifer all that well," Greg recalls, "but she called me and said that she had had a dream about me. She said it was important.

"She said that she and I, along with a third man, had ascended a flight of stairs in a very old hotel. She felt it had been some time in the days of the Old West. We had entered a room with the number eighteen on the door.

"Inside, a man dressed in black had served up shot glasses filled with Jack Daniels whiskey. He and I had drunk a toast."

Later, in thinking about the dream, Greg wondered whether T. J. Wright, the deceased gambler, hadn't been welcoming a partner into the hotel.

"That's the way I thought of it," Greg says. "I accepted Mr. Wright as a partner of mine, hoping there would be no arguments. I think it's worked out well, so far."

One of the previous owners, Pat Loree, had had more than one clash with the ghost of Mr. Wright.

"We didn't like each other," Pat recalls. "Something always happened when I went in there. I was even knocked to the floor once. We didn't get along at all."

Greg says there are times when even he isn't welcome in the room.

"I can recall touring the hotel with a psychic. I hadn't told her anything about the hotel, but when we got to Room Eighteen, she gravitated right to the door. She put her hands on the knob and the wood, and the hair stood up on my arms and neck. As they say, my skin crawled.

"She wanted in, so I placed the key in the lock. Try as I might, I couldn't get the lock to open. I thought I had the wrong key. The next morning I tried it again, and it opened right up."

Besides the gambler, Mary Lambert, the wife of the hotel's builder in 1880, is said to walk the halls and inhabit a room. She is reputed to be much more subtle than T.J. Wright, leaving only a wake of fragrant perfume.

It is also said that the ghost of a dwarf or small child inhabits the hotel, causing mischief. Letters, pens, and other office items will end up missing or mysteriously misplaced. The kitchen help often face cleanup after jars and dishes fall on their own from the shelves.

"They don't just fall off the edge," one cleaning woman comments. "They are pushed. We've stood and watched them go. I've seen it."

A fifteen-year-old cleaning boy saw the small ghost sitting on a bar stool, laughing at him. The boy quit his job that day.

Many have reported hearing the sounds of gatherings and parties in segments of the bar and lobby, usually during the very late hours. When someone goes to investigate, he or she finds nothing. The noise had died, only to resume when the person leaves again.

Very recently, a filmmaker came to the St. James to make a documentary. Though he saw nothing while filming, it was reported that while he was viewing his work on video, he saw two red eyes in a number of the rooms.

The St. James Hotel has always had a strong link to the past, a link that has never been broken through the chain of various owners. The hotel could double as a museum, with pictures and memorabilia everywhere. The feeling of the area's history is in every room.

Many famous historical figures have passed through the rooms and halls of the hotel, including Wyatt Earp, Bat Masterson, Wild Bill Hickok, Buffalo Bill, and Calamity Jane. As the hotel was a major stop on the Sante Fe Trail, many travelers into the Southwest found a place of rest there.

Others met their deaths. Gunfighters known to have stayed at the St. James include Clay Allison and Bob Ford, who history says was the killer of Jesse James. In all, twenty-six people have died of gunshot wounds in the hotel.

To Greg Champion, it is all a part of the local color.

"I think it's exciting. I know it's real, and I can't explain it, but I enjoy it. I guess as long as my partnership with T.J. Wright holds up, things should go very well."

OLD TRAILS
AND
GHOST TOWNS

11

The Mysteries of Old Garnet

Garnet, Montana
Northern Rocky Mountains

In the mountains west of Missoula, Montana, lies a ghost town where, some say, the past refuses to die.

Born during the gold rush of the 1860s, Garnet was a rough-and-tumble mining town. The strike was rich, and its reputation grew. By the 1880s, there were more than four thousand men there, working hard by day and drinking hard by night. It was one of the many large ore strikes in Montana Territory, and frontier trails led from other mining gulches to this high-mountain gold camp, which rests in a glen at an elevation of 5,800 feet.

The boomtown was a haven for gamblers and gold seekers, adventurers and thrill-seekers from every walk of life. There were stores and hotels and barber shops and, of course, a good number of saloons. Those honky-tonks were the scene of continuous partying, as miners would bring in their gold and immediately spend it on drink and women. Garnet, during its heyday, never lacked for excitement.

Nearly a century passed, and Garnet began to fall into ruin. The old wooden, false-fronted buildings began to sag and collapse. Age and weather were slowly bringing the past to decay, and a once thriving mining town was settling into the dust.

Helping this natural process along was the ongoing vandalism, theft, and the occasional fire that destroyed irreplaceable relics. The history of the area would soon be lost forever.

Then the Bureau of Land Management, using money allocated for historical restoration projects, undertook to put old Garnet back on its feet as a tourist stop. The buildings were restored and the signs repainted. Weeds were pulled and the streets cleared of debris. After a few years of remodeling and rebuilding, the gold town of Garnet took on new life. It also took on some old life.

One man who can attest to the latter was a fire-control chief and caretaker named Kerry Moon, who spent three summers and one winter in the mid-1970s working for the Bureau of Land Management. Moon managed a fire-fighting crew during the summer months and spent the winter months guarding the restored town against vandalism and thievery. Old Garnet never rested, Moon said. The old town would quiet down when the tourists were there, but it never really died.

"You could hear activity in the town almost any time of day," Moon says. "During daylight you could hear the sound of horses and men and wagons, regular activity that would have taken place back then. At nights, especially for some reason on Wednesdays, you could hear the sounds of partying—singing and dancing and laughing, lights in windows, and even honky-tonk music."

Moon mentioned that other members of the fire crew

noticed the noise as well and even complained occasionally that they were having trouble getting enough sleep. But not one of them was going to write a report that stated there were ghost parties taking place in the dance halls and saloons of a town vacant for more than fifty years.

"We decided we were going to have to get used to it," Moon remembers. "None of us had gone crazy. We just all realized that whatever was here when these people were alive brought them back in death."

Moon tells of how his dog would bark and growl, and how the hair would rise on its back. This happened so often that Moon became used to it. When the fire crew left for the winter, and Moon found himself in Garnet alone, the activity picked up considerably.

He has spent considerable time speculating on the reason.

"I don't know if it was because all the tourists were gone or because winter keeps people indoors up here, but the ghostly activity really increased. Somebody was knocking on my door almost every night, and there was a lot of noise downtown, almost continuous noise. I got so I just had to ignore it and do my work."

As he grew more used to the unusual phenomena, Moon found himself growing more curious about them. He got used to the fact that the knocks on the doors and windows were made by those who never left footprints in the snow, and he finally realized that there was nothing he could do to change any of it. He needed the job; the ghosts of old Garnet could have their way.

"I think the worst thing was the forge in the blacksmith shop," Moon recalls, speaking of the building where the horseshoes were made and the harnesses fixed. "I would hear that heavy pounding and think someone was in there fooling around. Then I would realize there was no one up here but me."

There were times when Moon would go down to get his work done and the activity would stop. He would go back up toward his cabin and sneak through the trees on the hillside and then just sit and listen.

"That's when I would hear the most activity going on," Moon relates. "It would be like they didn't know I was there and they would be going on with their activities just as if they were alive."

Moon remembers the first time he went to investigate the honky-tonk music that was coming from the middle of town. That winter in Garnet was incredibly harsh. Moon found himself chopping wood constantly to keep the little stove in his cabin producing heat. He had to go out to the highway in a snowmobile to pick up provisions and get his mail. When conditions weren't suitable for snowmobiling, he was forced to use cross-country skis or snowshoes, pulling a toboggan to pile supplies on.

During one storm, the snow was piling up deep. The wind blew almost constantly, and drifts filled in the streets and partially covered many of the buildings. Moon was spending his time reading and writing letters, then feeding the stove and himself. The mountain peaks were socked in by snow clouds, and the timber was coated a bleak white. He began to wonder why he had taken on this assignment.

On that morning of the big storm, he was chopping wood and thinking about nothing in particular. The flakes were fine and crystalline, and sparkled in the bitter cold. As he chopped he heard faint music from somewhere down in old Garnet. Faint, so faint, but music indeed.

Moon laid the ax down and raised his head to listen. Above the howl of the wind and driven snow he could hear the sound of a piano. A honky-tonk piano.

He began to feel a chill that was not brought on by the winter cold. He no longer noticed the snow that fell and melted against his face. He stared down the hill at the main street of Garnet.

Who could possibly be up here in this weather? And why would they want to be playing a piano?

He wondered if there might be skiers or snowmobilers in the area on a lark. But he had seen nobody and had heard no snow machines.

Maybe he hadn't even heard the music.

He began to chop wood again. But the sound persisted. Piano music was coming up through the storm from somewhere down in Garnet.

Finally, he decided his job dictated that he investigate what was going on. If people were up here, they could do a lot of damage, and he would have to answer for not having stopped them. He took his rifle and made his way through the snow into the center of the ghost town. He walked slowly on his snowshoes, stopping occasionally to listen. The wind came up and skimmed snow from the tops of drifts and whistled in the cracks of the old buildings. But the music was still clear.

It came from the Kelly Saloon, from behind the boarded-up walls and doors of the old drinking and gambling parlor. But there was no way to see inside.

Moon decided to go around back, where the saloon abutted a bank. In the early days, the saloon's second floor could be reached by placing a wood plank across from the cut bank to the second-story balcony. Looking up, Moon could see a snow-covered plank already laid across to the door on the upper story.

After listening again, he labored up the snowy slope and began to slowly work his way across the creaky, slippery plank. The music continued, changing to different songs now and again. When he was halfway across the plank, the music stopped.

He became frightened. He worked to calm himself, to

keep from slipping off the plank and breaking an arm or leg. Finally, he got back to the hill and took a deep breath, wiping wet snow from his face. Then the music started up again.

He wondered what he should do. Again he decided he had to see who or what the source of the music was. Once more he started across the plank to the rear door on the second story of the building, his rifle ready.

After working his way across—this time the music continued playing—he hesitated in front of the door. He reached out to brush snow off the doorknob. The balcony floor creaked beneath him and he grabbed hold of a support beam. The boards were sagging, and he worried as much now about falling through as he did about what he might see when he finally opened the door. When he did reach for the door, the music once again stopped.

With his rifle ready, he opened the door anyway and stepped slowly inside. He was in an upstairs hallway that led to bedrooms. It was dark and eerie, made even more desolate by the whistling of the storm through aged cracks and splintered wood. A number of startled pigeons flapped from roosting places and found their way through a broken window and out into the storm.

The pigeons scared him, and when he finally regained his composure, he thought more about turning around and leaving than moving ahead. After hesitating, he went on to where a stairway led down to the main floor.

The big room was vacant, with only the wind moaning in its curious way. He could see his breath and hear his heart thumping as he stood still and let his eyes grow used to the darkness. There certainly was no one there and hadn't been anyone there. But what bothered him most was to see that there was no piano whatsoever.

Since that time, Kerry Moon has taken other jobs and now lives in California. He has often wondered what it was about Garnet that brought back the past in such a strong way, a way that seems unlikely ever to die.

One theory is that the minerals in the area have preserved, or recorded, the life that once existed there. The mountains are filled with quartz, garnet, amethyst, and pyrites in a number of forms. It is thought that the crystals may possibly have something to do with the energy that haunts Garnet.

Crystals, especially quartz, are known to have strong properties that unify the four basic elements in nature: air, water, fire, and earth. As crystals are the bond of creation and link the earth and its inhabitants with the mysteries of the supernatural, it stands to reason that the crystals around Garnet would harbor the spirits of its long-dead inhabitants.

Whatever the reason for the ghostly dances and the sounds of everyday life that come from another plane in old Garnet, the fact is that the town still lives in the past. Depending on the sensitivity of the individual, much can be heard and seen. Ghosts of the Old West linger and reach out to those who wish to touch them.

12

La Llorona—
The Weeping Woman

The Santa Fe River
The Spanish Southwest Country

Patricio Lujan loved the violin. He was eighty-four years old when he played at Rancho de las Golondrinas in Santa Fe, New Mexico. As a much younger man, Patricio raised cattle between Mora and Guadalupita. The days and nights usually passed without incident; families would get together mainly to gossip and tell of the day's events. But there was one late afternoon sometime in the early 1930s that Patricio remembers vividly, an afternoon that still gives him shivers.

"There is a little creek that comes from Guadalupita," Patricio says. "We were sitting by the house, gossiping and talking, when all of a sudden we saw a woman. No one knew her and it gave me the chills."

The woman they saw was tall and thin, and dressed in white. Patricio and his family watched her as she crossed the bottom of a ravine not far away and walked onto Lucero Road.

"She got to the spot where she had to cross the river,"

Patricio recalls. "She just seemed to float over the water. Then she started going up the hill, and when she got to the top she disappeared into thin air. At a distance of about five hundred yards she reappeared. We watched her until she disappeared for the second time."

Patricio and his family were stunned by the incident. They went out to the road where she had passed and found she had left no footprints. There was no question in their minds that they had seen the woman called *La Llorona.*

Among the Hispanic people of the Southwest, *La Llorona* is a manifestation that has been with them since the days of the conquistadores. She is a bearer of sorrow, the frightful Weeping Woman who is seen from time to time along all the major rivers throughout the desert country. Her wailing cannot be mistaken, and the vision of her is one never forgotten.

The story of *La Llorona* is a tragic one. It is said she was a young woman blessed with natural beauty and born a peasant. She was unusually tall and had flowing black hair. Her beauty captured the fancy of the richer class, and the young men waited for her to appear when darkness fell. She lived her days among the poor, but by night turned herself into the beautiful señorita in white.

It is said she had two small sons who burdened her, making it difficult for her to spend her nights at the fandangos, where she was admired by everyone who saw her. This attention was more important to her than the care of her children, and as the story goes, the two small boys drowned in the river, either through neglect or by her own hand.

From the time of their deaths the beautiful *La Llorona* mourned her sons night and day. She could be seen in her white gown walking the banks of the river, searching for them, hoping they might come back to her. Her wailing was constant and she took no nourishment. Her gown became soiled and torn, and her tall frame appeared even taller as she grew thinner. Finally, when almost a skeleton, she died on the banks of the river.

Not long after, it was said that *La Llorona* reappeared. How could that be? She was dead. But her spirit could not rest. It was seen often by many, walking the banks of the river when darkness fell. Her wailing became a curse of the night. There were those who said they saw her drifting among the trees along the shore, or crossing the water just above the surface. Others spoke of seeing her floating in the current, crying out as her long white gown spread out upon the waters.

The people became afraid to go out at night. No one knew where she might appear next, for she was seen along many rivers now, across the entire Southwest. Mothers kept their children in, for it was said *La Llorona* would take them, that some had already been taken, lost in the river.

The legend of *La Llorona* has become part of Hispanic culture throughout the world. It is said she is everywhere now, and those who do not take care of their children will see her and she will teach them a lesson.

Among the Hispanic people of Santa Fe who know *La Llorona* well is Edward Garcia Kraul. Kraul, together with his wife, Judith Beatty, has turned his undivided attention to researching the legend of the Weeping Woman and has even named his house La Casa de La Llorona. For you see, the house the Krauls live in is the very same one that Patricio Lujan and his family lived in when *La Llorona* appeared to them on the road many years ago.

Kraul's involvement with the Weeping Woman does not stop there. In fact, many years before Patricio Lujan saw the ghost woman, Kraul's great uncle Epifanio Garcia encountered her while traveling with his brothers. The story demonstrates the sinister nature of the Hispanic spirit woman, who that day came to warn three young brothers against abusing their mother.

Epifanio was a precocious and outspoken boy. He argued not just with his mother but with his father as well. But the greatest hurt was toward his mother, who lived for him and wished the best for him. But Epifanio had a mind of his own and made his own decisions.

It was after an especially heated dispute that visibly distressed his mother that Epifanio decided to leave for a time. Accompanied by his brothers, Carlos and Augustine, he set out in a buckboard wagon for the Villa Real de Santa Fe, from their ranch in Ojo de La Vaca. After turning off on a branch of the old Santa Fe Trail toward the historic Apache Ridge area, at that time the Blas Garcia estate, Epifanio and his two brothers were visited by a tall woman from another dimension.

Ramana Martinez, Edward Kraul's great aunt, was a child at the time. She remembers hearing the story from the Garcia boys themselves and passing it on to Kraul's mother.

"Epifanio was driving the team, the horses, and Carlos was with him in front," she recalls. "Augustine, the youngest, was riding in the back. Epifanio and Carlos were talking when there suddenly appeared on the seat between them a very beautiful lady wearing a black *tapelo*. She had a black net over her face and wore silver earrings."

It was dusk and the three terrified boys could feel her much more than see her. Each boy in turn tried to talk to the phantom woman, each without success. She was there, with them, but she was silent. Epifanio continued to drive the horses, fearing that if he stopped something bad might happen.

She remained there until Epifanio finally turned the horses from the old Santa Fe Trail onto Garcia Street. Just before the wagon reached the street, the apparition dissolved. But not before Epifanio distinctly heard her speak to him.

"I will visit you again someday when you argue with your mother."

The youngest boy, Augustine, fainted.

The Weeping Woman has presented herself to many different people in many different ways over the years. Consider the terror experienced by a group of migrant Hispanic workers in the spring of 1954.

A woman named JoAnn who now makes her home in Santa Fe remembers the incident well. She was fifteen at the time and traveling from Las Vegas, New Mexico, to Avondale, Colorado, near Pueblo. She was with her husband, a brother-in-law, and a cousin. They were headed north to work in the fields. For JoAnn it was the most terrifying trip of her life.

"There were some houses that were loaned to the workers there," JoAnn recalls. "They called them *colonias,* to be used by the people working in the fields. They were away from the town. We stayed in a very long house, with three or four other families. Around twelve-thirty in the morning we heard this loud noise coming from the river—about half a mile away. It woke everyone up—not just in our house but in all of the surrounding houses as well."

JoAnn remembers how everyone then ran outside. The cry was loud and shrill, and seemed quite close. The workers huddled together. There seemed little doubt that, for some reason, *La Llorona* had followed them.

JoAnn's husband and some other men got into cars to investigate. They had bright spotlights, which they turned on as they drove toward the river. While the crying continued, JoAnn and the others watched the men as they crossed a bridge. But when they got to the other side of the river, the wailing seemed to be coming from the opposite shore.

"This happened about four times, this crossing the river back and forth," JoAnn relates. "Then it stopped as suddenly as it started. But now there was another sound."

The workers heard it coming from the little chapel just up from the river, near the cemetery.

"You know the sound of a football game, when you're in a big group of people and it sounds like the buzzing of bees?" JoAnn says. "This is the sound that came from the chapel in the pitch black night that *La Llorona* came. The buzzing lasted about a half hour, then it stopped. The next day we went to the chapel to see if there was anything there, but there was no sign of anything."

JoAnn, her husband, and the rest of the workers could find no explanation for the strange terror that touched their lives that night. Many among them who had had previous experiences with *La Llorona* had no doubt it was she. None of them actually saw the tall Weeping Woman—for some reason she did not come in visible form—but her horrible cries identified her.

La Llorona has never settled in death; in fact, her wanderings grow ever wider. The tall Weeping Woman seems to go wherever Hispanic people go. Her movements have been traced throughout the region of the Southwest and now farther north.

Even today, days and nights in and around Santa Fe are never ordinary. Though the city is growing, it will never lose its identity as an Indian-Hispanic center of culture. The past has deep roots here, and when those roots are disturbed in any way, unexplained things seem to occur.

All of Santa Fe knows that one particular building in the downtown section—the PERA Building, which houses the Public Employees Retirement Association—is built on an old Spanish-Indian graveyard. It is an unusual building in its own right, as it was constructed with two stories underground and three above. In Santa Fe there is a long-standing city ordinance that prohibits any building reaching higher than the cathedral, and for this reason, the PERA Building is built partially underground.

The building is near the Santa Fe River, the traditional haunting grounds of *La Llorona,* and for that reason many Hispanics will not go near it. Those who have been employed there, especially janitors and night watchmen, tell of hearing cries and loud noises resounding through the halls. Others say the stairways are dangerous, for unseen hands have been known to reach out and push.

Among those who have witnessed firsthand unexplained occurrences in the building is Henrietta Stockel, who at one time worked there. She remembers how in the summer of 1981 she came in contact with someone in the building who may have been *La Llorona.*

"I used to work on the third floor in the copy room," she recalls. "There were two elevators and I was just out from them, working with my back to them most of the day. I was often copying one thing or another when other employees would come out of the elevators to get something. They would say something in greeting and I would get used to their voices. But then one afternoon, while I was working alone, something strange happened."

She heard one of the elevators open. But whoever came out didn't say anything. She turned to see who it was just in time to see a filmy figure glide around the corner.

"I was startled," she recalls. "But I went around the corner to see what it was. There, moving down the hall, was a tall, very thin figure of what appeared to be a woman. She was dressed in a long, flowing gown that appeared almost grayish. I watched her turn the corner again. Then I walked down there, but she was gone."

Henrietta Stockel will never be quite sure who it was she saw that afternoon in the hall of the PERA Building. It might have been the legendary *La Llorona* or it might have been a wandering spirit exiled by the disinterment of the graves. But it is an experience she will never forget.

No one can forget the timeless woman who wanders the rivers of the Southwest looking for her children. She has had such a great impact on the Hispanic people that there is no place they can go where she does not appear to someone. In fact, the migration of Hispanics as far north as Billings, Montana, has brought *La Llorona* to the banks of the Yellowstone River, where some have seen her wandering through the cottonwoods there.

"She is here, just as she has always been with our people," a man named Juan says. "There are those who have seen her here and have become frightened. We have come up here to work in the beet fields, and she watches us. There was a glass figurine that showed up in an antique shop—it was she. The lady did not remember where the beautiful glass figure had come from, and she did not know of *La Llorona,* but she did not laugh at us. She seemed to understand."

It is said among the Hispanic people that the Weeping Woman will always be with them. They feel she will never stop following the many rivers to look for her children. For this reason the darkness holds for them a special fear that is passed from generation to generation. The cries of the Weeping Woman, the spirit they call *La Llorona,* are never still. They will continue forever.

13

Night of the Iron Horse

Sinks of Dove Creek—Kelton, Utah
Near Golden Spike National Historic Site

In May 1869, the Great Basin of Utah was the scene of one of western history's most noted achievements—the completion of the transcontinental railroad. A multitude of laborers, primarily Chinese on the Central Pacific side, had succeeded in bringing locomotion across the vast expanses of the West.

The efforts of both sides culminated at Promontory City, thereafter named Promontory Point, Utah. On that day the crowd cheered and the bands played while gold spikes were pounded into a laurel tie with a silver-headed sledgehammer by dignitaries from both the Union and Central Pacific Railroads. A telegraph wire was attached to the last spike, and from this remote location a message was sent that said the East and West Coasts of the burgeoning United States of America were at last linked.

Celebrations began in all the major cities from coast to

coast. Locomotives and fire engines lined up everywhere to sound long, smoky blasts. In New York City, Wall Street suspended business while a hundred guns fired continuous salutes in City Hall park. Flags were hoisted everywhere in Philadelphia, and bells at Independence Hall and in all the churches chimed. An impromptu parade seven miles long clogged the city of Chicago, while the cities of Sacramento and San Francisco celebrated in similar fashion throughout the night.

And when it was finally over, and the headlines and the oratory had faded, the workers themselves faded from the saloons and dance halls of Promontory City. They left their tent camps along the grade and went to seek other work, or perhaps their fortunes in the rapidly expanding gold fields of the northern Rocky Mountains.

Many of the Chinese laborers made their way back to the West Coast. One of their primary encampment sites, at the site of the Sinks of Dove Creek, was abandoned. For more than a hundred years since the feverish laying of track, the old labor camp at Sinks of Dove Creek has been abandoned to the vast reaches of desert all around.

Or maybe it only appears to have been abandoned. There are those who question that. Some feel that an impression in time exists there, or that perhaps lost spirits of dead laborers have returned to fill the energy they created in building the railroad. Whatever it is, something is there.

One who knows that to be true is Steve Ellison, a historian and park ranger now stationed at a prominent historic site in the West. Ellison is well versed in the history of the West and deals in facts. But an experience at Sinks of Dove Creek on a night in September 1979 led him to believe that facts are not always what they seem in the human mind.

That night convinced him that there is more to be seen and felt than can be explained. He wonders now if the workers from long ago have somehow made their way back to their old work camp—and that their energy may be keeping the old Central Pacific locomotives active still.

"It sounds really crazy, I know," Ellison says of his experience. "And it scared me to the point that my knees were literally knocking together. But I will swear it happened."

A treacherous county road now occupies the old Central Pacific Railroad grade that once supported ties and rails for the trains that crossed the Great Basin. Steve and a number of friends, out on a historic reenactment march, set up their tents at the site of the abandoned work camp at Sinks of Dove Creek. All the marchers were dressed in authentic army uniforms, similar to those worn by members of the Twenty-first Infantry, assigned to protect the workers.

Ellison was walking the 2:00 A.M. to 5:00 A.M. guard shift along the old grade above the encampment. It had been unusually warm for that time of year and the high desert was still simmering from the day's sun. The men were exhausted from the long march and were all sleeping soundly.

"There was no moon," Ellison recalls. "But the stars were bright and they seemed close enough to touch. I can remember patrolling along the grade with my rifle over my shoulder and looking down at the campfires and the tents along the bottom. It was very still and the light flickered against the rows of tents. I couldn't help thinking that this must have been exactly how things were back in 1869 when the transcontinental was being laid here. Then, suddenly, everything didn't seem quite right to me."

He heard a sound in the distance. He remembers it as being like the muffled roar of a rocket. The night was otherwise still, and he knew the sound wasn't wind. He strained to see what was coming, but could make out only a small light that appeared to be swinging from side to side, until it moved off the grade and down into the brush.

Then the muffled roar became a *chug-chug* sort of sound that kept coming closer and closer. A *chug-chug-chug-chug* that increased in intensity. There were no lights except the small dancing light that had appeared to be a lantern. The sound held his attention.

"I was sort of rooted there," he explains. "I was terrified and couldn't move. I couldn't see anything at all, but I could hear the sound coming straight at me. Then this sound seemed to rush up over me in a kind of blast, soaring right over my head. I couldn't believe it."

In a panic, he made his way back into camp. He stayed near the fire in front of his tent, looking all around him in the darkness. He couldn't control the shaking and trembling of his body, and he wondered if he was going to have a nervous breakdown.

Finally he got himself under control. He knew he couldn't wake up the next guard, because he wasn't due on duty for at least a couple of hours. Ellison resolved that he would go back up on the grade and stick out his time.

After convincing himself there was nothing there that could hurt him, he climbed back onto the old railroad grade, slung his .45–70 Springfield rifle back onto his shoulder, and began to walk his sentry path. That's when the footsteps and the whispering started.

"At first I couldn't make out for sure what it was," he recalls. "I began to get scared again, but reminded myself I couldn't leave my post. Finally, when I had settled down again, I listened carefully. There were voices, distinct voices. I came to the conclusion that they were Chinese."

While he listened, he could make out snatches of conversation. He could repeatedly hear the words *A-melican, A-melican,* and once again the hair stood up on his neck and arms.

"It seemed like those voices had followed me from somewhere," he says. "Then I remembered San Francisco, where I had spent the summer a year before. My Chinese landlady would always refer to Caucasians as 'A-melicans.' Every white person was an 'A-melican.' Whoever was on that railroad grade that night had to have been Chinese."

Ellison realized that the soldiers of the Twenty-first Infantry, assigned to protect the workers back in 1869, were likely referred to as "A-melicans" by the Chinese laborers. Apparently, Steve Ellison was standing in the historic past.

He became convinced nothing was going to happen to him. As he began to relax, he could hear more voices and feel the constant bustle of men working around him. He heard dull thuds that seemed far away, as if they were coming from somewhere beneath the ground, and decided it must be the spikes being hammered into the rails. He heard the patter of small footsteps—the Chinese carried water on long poles over their shoulders—and the heavier footfalls of the bigger Irish, German, and other European men working with the Chinese. And as he stared down the grade into the blackness, Ellison remembers seeing something else.

"It was a multitude of tiny pinpricks of light, like sparks flying from the spikes and rails. It was as if a hundred men were pounding all at once. I just settled down and realized that the past was being relived in phantom form."

The next morning he discussed the events of the night with the others on the outing. Few questioned his experience, and many even talked about things they had seen or felt or heard at other sites around the West. Some of them expressed disappointment that he hadn't awakened them to share in the experience.

"It was the first time something like that had happened to me," Ellison says. "I thought sure everyone would consider me crazy. Who could have believed all that?"

As he later learned, there were any number of people who

would certainly have "believed all that." The old Central Pacific grade has been the center of eerie stories through the years. People who hunt in the area know of the strange sounds and noises, and of the locomotive ghost train that still rides the old grade on invisible rails. Those who know the area and are aware of its legacy avoid it. That is why the road remains in disrepair. No one wants to travel where a ghost train might run them down. And if that isn't enough to bring fear, the voices and the noise of phantom workers is.

Though few will talk openly about it, many look at one another and understand. Before the tracks were dismantled, stories were told in private among engineers concerning strange trains coming at them on their runs through the desert. These engineers will attest that some of these ghost trains even had lights along with the noise, terrifying lights that meant one thing: another train was coming. It always astonished the conductors and engineers, for they knew there couldn't be any other trains on this line. It was something they never forgot.

The experiences were similar. The engineers would see the lights and try to come to a stop. But even if they could stop, the other train would keep on coming. Then the light and the energy and the sound would pass right through their solid engines.

And the workers? The local people won't talk about them—they don't like to admit they can hear people they cannot see. They don't like to think they hear the voices of people who have died.

But the sounds and voices are there at Sinks of Dove Creek. When Steve Ellison and his companions walked around their camping area, they found numerous dugouts filled with weeds and brush that had once been the underground parts of Chinese labor huts. The hair on Ellison's neck and arms again tingled.

"I could feel them there as well," he remembers, "coming and going, moving around me. Some of the others said they could feel them, too. We didn't know what to do, so we just left."

Ellison says that the entities at Sinks of Dove Creek seemed to be lost, to have been wandering around doing things they had in life, not realizing they should have crossed over by now. Some may argue that it wasn't actually the spirits themselves but some physical pattern left behind, some energy that keeps playing over and over.

But Ellison has reason to believe they may be wandering souls who feel they haven't completed their work. He says the more he opened up, the more he felt the presence of strong emotion and determination, something left in the environment from the rush of the workers to finish the line. He felt as if they needed some form of release and couldn't find it.

"I felt sad for them," Ellison says. "I even prayed for them at times."

Whether or not the prayers will do them any good is anybody's guess. Some may benefit and find where they should be, while others may linger on, working and waiting for the rush of the phantom engines that ride the invisible tracks past Sinks of Dove Creek.

14

The Cabin in Brown's Park

Brown's Park
Northwestern Colorado

Named after fur trapper Baptiste Brown, Brown's Hole—as it was first known—began as a place where mountain men rendezvoused, and later where trail-worn longhorns were pastured for the winter. It was well known for its unusually open winters, whereas the rest of the Rocky Mountain region was normally buried in snow and cold.

When the range-cattle industry grew in the West, large herds were pastured year-round. It was during that period that a well-bred Southern lady insisted the valley be called a "park," not a "hole," for she considered the country far more beautiful than that. She succeeded, and the rugged piece of back country took the name Brown's Park.

When the cattle industry flourished, Brown's Park was the scene of rancher feuds and range wars. Blood was spilled, and it became known as dangerous country. Men on the run from the law were a common sight, and Brown's Park became a stopover on the notorious Outlaw Trail.

Today the valley retains its beauty and its legend. It is said that some of those who rode through here, and perhaps even those who died here, may have never left.

Don Coldsmith, a writer from Emporia, Kansas, can attest to that. Tall and formidable, Coldsmith writes Western novels about the heart of the frontier. He does not look to be a man easily shaken. But an otherwise calm winter afternoon in late December 1983 left Coldsmith wondering if there are powers from the past we cannot explain.

Coldsmith was traveling in a pickup with his son-in-law, Mike, who then managed a large cattle operation along the Green River. The cattle were out on winter pasture and it was time to check how far they had strayed from their home range.

Checking for cattle on acreage as vast as Brown's Park is a job that demands a lot of driving and riding, searching continuously with binoculars for stray cattle that might be anywhere. On this day, Coldsmith and his son-in-law discovered some stray livestock that needed herding back toward the home range. It was the beginning of a strange afternoon.

Coldsmith looked over the vast country while Mike spotted cattle through his binoculars. Mike said matter-of-factly, "Looks like they've drifted over near Butch's place." He was searching the slopes near a run-down cabin just above the Green River.

Coldsmith asked what "Butch's place" meant. He was told that the locals who know the history say the cabin was a frequent hideout spot for Butch Cassidy and his Wild Bunch.

"You know, the outlaw Butch Cassidy?" Mike said.

Of course Coldsmith knew of Butch Cassidy. Most everybody, Western writer or not, had heard of the famous outlaw once portrayed by actor Paul Newman.

Coldsmith was already growing excited. "I certainly know who you mean. It's just amazing that we would be near a cabin once occupied by the Wild Bunch."

There was little question in Coldsmith's mind that the cabin was likely what the locals said it was—a remnant of the old Outlaw Trail and one-time hangout for one of the most notorious gangs the West had ever known. The Wild Bunch had spent a lot of time in Brown's Park, right in this area of the deep back country.

Coldsmith thought that now he was going to get a first-hand view of history. An old gun, or even a shell casing, would be a great souvenir. There had to be something there that he could take home to show he had been in Butch Cassidy's cabin.

Mike was smiling. He knew his father-in-law was anxious to inspect the cabin more closely, but there were cows to move and that work had to be done.

After a ten-mile drive upstream to a rickety suspension bridge, Coldsmith was thinking more and more about the old cabin and its wild history. He helped Mike fold down the side mirrors on the pickup so that they could clear the cables on the sides of the bridge. Once across, Mike drove the pickup along a rutted trail filled with boulders. Finally they reached the vicinity of the cabin.

Near an isolated corral, Mike whistled and scattered oats from a coffee can on the tailgate of the pickup. Two horses appeared and trotted over. They both ate oats while Mike bridled and saddled one. He swung up on the horse and pointed down the river.

"Take the pickup down if you want," he said. "The cabin is about a mile and off to the left. I'll bunch these cows and see you later."

The cabin was on a rise overlooking the river. Coldsmith walked through the grass and looked around: the location was perfect for a cabin whose occupants wanted a good view of the area. Anyone riding anywhere near this place could be seen easily long before they arrived. He stood near the cabin and looked into the vast country of rolling foothills and red cliffs, which pushed into a wall of rising mountains. Seeing a posse from a good distance could give them time to decide whether to run or fight.

The cabin was weathered and most of the roof had caved in. Coldsmith strolled through the ruins for a time, considered the events that had happened and the stories that had been told here. It was intriguing to think Butch Cassidy had called this place home. Standing in the doorway, Coldsmith felt the peace and contentment of the wilderness. The area had not changed since the days of the Wild Bunch.

While watching an antelope that had wandered nearby, he realized he was seeing what the outlaws had seen so many years before. He began to feel almost as if he were back there. He leaned against the door frame with his left shoulder and raised his right hand to place against the opposite side of the door. As he touched the door frame with his hand, he felt as if he had activated a switch.

Something he would never be able to explain was suddenly happening to him. It was as if someone or something had entered his body.

There was now a presence within him, something undefined that seemed to be looking out at the river through his eyes. It was an invading presence, but a contented one. A different consciousness was now somehow within him.

In that unusual moment, Don Coldsmith felt that he was someone else.

It took a few moments for him to recover his own consciousness. Something had suddenly happened, and just as suddenly was gone. Though it was unnerving to a degree, it was not threatening. Instead, it was a feeling more of comfort and relaxation—as if someone from the past was once again enjoying the cabin in Brown's Park, through his senses.

He will always insist that *someone* besides him was there that day. Whoever it was—Butch Cassidy or another outlaw—had stood in that doorway before, slouching comfortably in the same position Coldsmith had assumed accidentally.

Butch Cassidy was released from the Wyoming Penitentiary in the spring of 1896. It is said that he returned immediately to Brown's Park with some of the old gang, and took up residence.

One of Cassidy's close associates was a man named Matt Warner, who had a cabin along the Green River, not far from Lodore. Warner's intention was to create a horse ranch; but with Butch back, robbing banks and trains was a better way to make fast money.

Warner, in later years, documented his days with the Wild Bunch. In his book *Last of the Bandit Riders,* Warner talks about the cabin. He writes:

> As I fixed it up, and stocked it with horses, it became more and more the headquarters of my old outlaw and half-outlaw pals. Eliza Lay, who became a real outlaw after I left that section, and Charlie Crouse, good-hearted old cattle rustler from Brown's Park; and finally Cassidy heard I was back, and came to live with me. My cabin was crowded every night by a drinking, poker-playing, bragging crowd.

With the passing of time, Brown's Park remains the same: the rising peaks that surround the vast valley are unchanged, as is the Green River bottomland that is still winter pasture for livestock. This valley will forever hold the legend of the Outlaw Trail and the men who rode it. It is part of the heritage of the Old West that will never die. Though the hoofprints of stolen horses have long since been erased by time, and the cabins have fallen to wind and weather, the memories of those who were there, in some form we cannot understand, will always be alive.

15

The Wolf Girl
of Texas

Devil's River
Del Rio, Texas

In the brush country, there is a legend that tells a strange tale of a wolf girl. But what began merely as a legend from deep in the last century seems to have somehow entered a realm beyond the ordinary, a dimension the human mind can't yet understand.

Jim Marshall of Dallas, an avid bowhunter and hiker, remembers how he and two friends encountered something in the fall of 1974 that none of them could explain or understand. It was there and then it was gone—it was there and gone again. The experience left them shaken and convinced that the open spaces of Texas can bring to the eyes visions that reach too far back into the mind to ever get rid of.

"I knew the story about the wolf girl of Devil's River," Marshall says, "but I thought it was just that, a story. What we saw that evening couldn't have been just our imaginations playing tricks on us. We all three saw the same thing."

Marshall and his friends were hunting javelina, the small peccaries, or wild pigs, that roam the southwestern desert country. They were camped along Devil's River, and after four days of solid hunting were becoming tired.

"I remember we had a fire going and the sun was just down," Marshall recalls. "One of my friends said he was going to get some firewood. He had no sooner left camp than he ran back, his face drained white."

They asked him what was wrong and he said they had better see for themselves, otherwise they would never believe him. The three of them went out from camp along the river to where a well-used trail went down to the water. They stopped and looked around while the first hunter told Marshall and the other hunter what he had seen, since there didn't appear to be anything there now. While he was describing it, Marshall saw something on the opposite shore that stood watching them.

"The only way I can describe it," he says, "is that it appeared to be a girl, a real skinny girl, with long hair and wild eyes. Even in the darkness we could see her. It was like she was in a haze, a kind of foggy mist, standing there partly bent over, digging into an ant mound. Suddenly whatever we were seeing was gone. I don't know if it vanished or just moved quickly into the brush. I was scared and my mind started to clamp up on me."

When the three men had recovered their breath, they returned to camp and immediately set to taking down their tent and packing up to leave. They worked fast, glancing around them and keeping three large lamps lit. They didn't stop driving until they reached Del Rio.

The legend of the wolf girl of Devil's River tells of an infant girl raised by wolves who spent her life hunting with a pack until she disappeared and was never seen again. Some say she was shot, while others say no one knows what happened to her. But there is evidence that the wolf girl lived on the Plains.

The legend began at the time of the Texas Revolution and a colony named after John Charles Beals. The colony sprang up at Delores, Texas, in 1834 and quickly fell prey to drought and fear of Santa Anna's marching army. It was unfortunate for those colonists who fled north along the Presido Road, for they found themselves in the heart of the Comanche nation. Most were butchered and left on the prairie to rot.

Just before all of this, a woman named Mollie Pertul Dent, with child, followed her husband up Devil's River from the colony to Beaver Lake to trap during the spring season. While there neither knew of Santa Anna or the flight of the colony into destruction. John Dent was busy trapping, while Mollie grew ever closer to her due date.

It is said that a girl was born to the couple in May 1835, while they were still on Devil's River. As the story goes, Mollie died in childbirth and John was either struck by lightning or otherwise killed while riding through a thunderstorm to reach the Pecos River and find help. Days after the birth, Mexican sheepherders found both John Dent's body and that of his wife. But there was no baby.

The baby was presumed dead, as wolf tracks all around Mollie's body showed that a pack had been attracted to her by the smell of blood. The bodies were buried and life went on, until nearly fourteen years later, when tales of strange sightings began to reach the campfires of the Mexican sheepherders and the wagon trains of the forty-niners bound for the gold fields. They spent their nights discussing what a Mexican boy claimed to have seen while tending a herd of goats.

It is said to have occurred near what is now Del Rio but was then called San Felipe Springs. The young Mexican sheepherder told of trying to drive off a pack of wolves that was attacking his flock. With them was what appeared to be a young woman with extremely long hair that covered her face and back, and a body with odd muscle development in the arms and shoulders.

The boy ran back to his village to report the sighting. He was not laughed at, for Seminole scouts working out of nearby Camp Hudson for the U.S. Army already refused to go into the Devil's River country. Some of the scouts had found hand- and footprints among the tracks of a pack of wolves. Super- stition or not, the scouts would not go near the river country after that.

Because so much was being made of this wolf girl along the river, a hunt was organized to see what truth there was to it. As the story goes, the hunters found the wolf pack and trapped it in a box canyon. The girl was captured with ropes while half screaming, half howling. She was examined and found to be human, but oddly proportioned from running on all fours for great lengths of time.

It is said the girl was then taken to a ranch house and locked in a bedroom under guard until it could be decided what would be done with her. Again she screamed and howled and brought the wolf pack into the brush just outside the ranch yard. Finally the pack attacked horses and cattle in a corral and brought the guards out to drive them away. The wolf girl went crazy and broke out. She was lost in the night with the wolf pack, and no other organized hunts could ever fool the pack again.

In years that followed there were reports from people who saw the girl suckling pups and attacking herds of sheep and goats with the wolf pack. But she would always escape deep into the Devil's River country and no amount of tracking could find her.

In 1852 a surveying crew laying out a new route to El Paso reported seeing what appeared to be the wolf girl with two pups on a sand bar in the middle of the river. Again the news spread that the Devil's River country was the source of one of the strangest stories ever to come out of Texas. But for a long while nothing else was heard about the wolf girl of Devil's River.

The legend seemed to have ended with the last sighting of the girl on the sand bar. But the story is confusing: some variations say that the survey crew, or a different one, succeeded in shooting the wolf girl, and then watched her disappear into the brush along the river. There is no way to confirm any reports of where the wolf girl was last seen.

But the story that Jim Marshall and his friends tell of the strange night during the javalina hunt suggests that the wolf girl might still roam the reaches of Devil's River in a form returned from the dead.

16

The Shadows in Scapponia Park

Northwestern Oregon

The area north of Portland, Oregon, is heavily forested and alive with beauty. Scapponia Park, a small, isolated campground on the east fork of the Nehalem River, is located just off Route 47, between Vernonia and Scappose.

The park is home to a strange mystery. There are some who say the pretty little spot harbors a fugitive from another time and place, an outlaw who wanders the shadowed woods after the sun goes down.

Henry Schlyper and his family, out on their very first camping trip, arrived at Scapponia Park late on a beautiful Sunday afternoon in May 1973.

"We had just gotten new sleeping bags and a tent," Henry remembers, "and we were all anxious to camp out for the night. Scapponia Park was only twenty miles from our home and we thought it the perfect place to go."

They arrived in a 1952 Willys Jeep, a rugged old four-wheeler that had taken them many places in the backcountry. That evening everyone jumped from the vehicle, eager to begin their night in the forest. They felt privileged, as they were the only campers in the park and could look forward to having the facilities all to themselves.

Maybe their being alone was the reason for what happened that night.

Henry remembers the events as if they had occurred only yesterday.

"We camped near a large oak tree. My wife and I put up the tent while our two young daughters explored nearby and helped gather firewood. We had a hard time with the tent, as there were a lot of unmarked poles, but we got it up as darkness was falling. Then we got the fire going and sat down to eat and listen to the wind rustle the tops of the firs."

Then something disturbing happened. The heat from the flames drove hoards of large black ants out of the trees.

"We hadn't seen ants like that before, and certainly none that size," Henry recalls. "They were everywhere."

As it was already late, they decided to go to bed. Henry kept the campfire going very low, to provide some light. Everyone fell asleep immediatley.

"I awakened around one A.M.," Henry remembers. "I looked out of the tent and saw the shadow of a man and his dog walking around the campsite. I worried that he might want to rob us and that we had no protection. I laid still and after five minutes they started off in the direction of the restrooms and disappeared under the big oak tree."

Henry fell asleep but awakened again an hour later. The man and his dog were back, wandering around the campsite.

"I had no idea who this was and what he was doing in the middle of nowhere," Henry says. "He might have been a transient who saw the campfire and hoped for a meal. But why did he remain at a distance and not make contact?"

Again the man and his dog walked toward the tree, suddenly disappearing completely. Henry lay in his sleeping bag a short time and awakened his wife, telling her they needed to leave immediatley, that he would explain later.

Henry remembers that he had never been so shaken before in his life.

"I tore that tent down real fast and just threw it in the back of the Jeep, without trying to fold it or anything. The girls asked why we had to leave so quickly, but they didn't argue."

Once everyone was in the Jeep, Henry turned over the ignition, but the engine wouldn't start. He had never had problems with the vehicle before and once the motor did start, it sputtered and backfired as they drove away.

Five miles down the road, he took a flashlight and adjusted the carburetor. Once back behind the wheel, he drove steadily, while his wife and daughters wondered what was troubling him.

They arrived home at three A.M. and after the girls were in bed and asleep, Henry explained everything to his wife, who had slept soundly through the whole thing.

At work on Monday, Henry sat in the break room with a cup of coffee when a co-worker joined him and asked about his weekend. Henry replied they had spent a night at Scapponia Park.

"Did you see the ghost and his dog?" the co-worker asked. Henry said he didn't believe in such things and the co-worker added, "There's one up there, they say. It's a horse thief who was hanged by a posse some time in the late 1800s. They say he lived in an old cabin there and that a posse dragged him out, shot his dog, and strung him up on that big oak in the middle of the campground. They say that two of them are buried together under that tree."

Henry Schlyper finished his coffee and went back to work, his outlook on life and its meaning changed forever. Despite urgings over the years from his wife and daughters to go back, he never returned to Scapponia Park. But whenever he sees a large oak tree, he remembers the shadowy figure of a man and his dog, wandering the outskirts of their campsite in the windy darkness of an eerie night he will never forget.

NATIVE
AMERICAN
SPIRITUALISM

17

The Mystery of the Little People

The Pryor Mountains
South-Central Montana

They have always existed in the stories and legends of the Absaroka Crow Indians, the small and powerful beings they call the Little People. Though other tribes fear and even despise them, to the Crow the Little People are protectors. They are powerful medicine. Whether they exist as flesh and blood or in spirit form is not important to them. What is important is that they exist.

The Little People have been protectors of the Crow for years, possibly even before the tribe moved into the intermountain west from the north-central part of the country. There are stories of how during the days of intertribal warfare the Little People would lay in wait for war parties, then rush out to tear the hearts out of their enemies' horses. The stories have been passed on from generation to generation, and at the Crow Medicine Rock in the Pryor Mountains of south-central Montana, offerings are still made to ask for help and success and healing in this life.

The Crow revere their past and the great men among them who have known the Little People. They had chiefs and medicine men to whom the Little People would come and bring medicine for healing and for war and for taking horses. Often the Little People would come to them in medicine dreams and promise to guide them if they would listen to them.

One of the most noted among these warriors of the last century was the great chief Plenty Coups. He was honored by the Little People while still a young man. In Plenty Coups's medicine dream he was led through the air from a high mountain by a spirit person who took him to a lodge and opened the entrance flap. Inside the lodge there was light, but no fire. The lodge was filled with warriors of various nations he did not recognize. But he knew they were warriors because each had a white coup stick lined with the "breath" feathers of a war eagle, the special tail feathers that the Indians believe carry the bird as silently as breath from the body.

Some of the warriors frightened Plenty Coups. They were dark warriors with missions to accomplish back in the earth life from which he had come. Their mission was to bring evil and to take with them into the dark pit below the people they could. Plenty Coups realized he could not stop these dark warriors from doing what they wished. He was to leave them alone. He had learned about them and now knew to avoid them.

Then a small person seated in the lodge handed Plenty Coups a number of breath feathers and told him how to count coups. The small warrior said he was from the Medicine Rock, where he and his people lived. They were the makers of the stone arrow points and lived throughout the mountains, enemies to some and allies to others. Everyone respected the Little People.

Then the small warrior told Plenty Coups and the others that someday Plenty Coups would become a great chief. He told Plenty Coups that his people, the Little People, would be his spirit helpers and that he must listen to them. Plenty Coups had challenges ahead of him and he must use the knowledge and talents the Creator gave him.

Plenty Coups awakened from his medicine dream drenched with sweat, but filled with great determination. He realized that a man must know himself before he knows others, and that whatever he accomplishes he does because *he* makes it happen. Plenty Coups, with the help of the Creator, was to use his talents to perform good among his people.

Plenty Coups went on to become the great chief the Little People warrior had predicted. It was during his time that most of the stories of the Little People circulated widely, including the tales of their incredible strength. One story tells how one of the Little People was seen moving a freshly killed elk toward the Medicine Rock with ease, merely by slipping the animal's head across his back and dragging the rest behind. It was said the Little People ate meat ravenously, for they had strong canine teeth.

There are also other stories, some of which show the Little People as tricksters when they are angered. People who try to catch them or attempt to play tricks on them are met with incredible supernatural powers that generally destroy the individual and often his or her entire family as well. The Crow have a great deal of respect for the Little People and generally avoid going into the Pryor Mountain area after dark. That is home to the Little People and the night is their own. This came first from Plenty Coups.

Plenty Coups was not only a great Crow leader, but a

renowned humanitarian as well. He is considered today to be one of the great men who lived during the last days of the Plains Indians, not only among the Crow but among all people who revere life and the good things that can be accomplished.

Today the Crow reservation is seeing the return of the old ways. The young people are learning what their forefathers had taught before the coming of the white man. Much of this knowledge is spreading into other cultures, whether Indian or white or any color. No power has ever been stronger than that of good, and people are discovering this as they try to solve the many problems they face.

The Crow know that the Little People are there helping them. It is said that when a Crow is going down the wrong path and knows better, he will meet one of the Little People standing with his arms crossed. The Little Person might not speak, but his message is always clear.

Most often the Little People come at night, usually into a bedroom where a sick person is being healed. Sometimes, when the man or woman has been behaving badly, the Little Person will stand on top of the bed at the foot with his arms crossed. Again, this means that a warning is being given.

Lorena Walks is a Crow woman who knows the Little People and what they can do. As a young woman of twenty she had a throat problem that caused her a great deal of pain and would have required disfiguring surgery to correct.

Somehow Lorena had swallowed a piece of toothpick and it became lodged in her lower throat. She had spent a couple of weeks trying to get it out by eating quantities of bread, but that only drove the toothpick deeper into the lining of the esophagus. Throat lozenges given to her by a doctor offered no relief. Soon she was to the point where she could not eat and could barely breathe.

At that time a medicine man named Dexter Williamson

Sr. was still alive. The Crow people loved him and thought of him as a holy man who gave of himself to help others. Lorena's father called on Dexter Williamson Sr. to help his daughter, and after he was offered the appropriate gifts, the old medicine man came to the home of the Walks family.

"It was winter and the sun was down early," Lorena recalls. "It was totally dark in the room—we lived in a one-room house—and all there was for light was a little glow of fire in the coal stove. Dexter wanted it that way. He wanted it dark."

Lorena became frightened when the medicine man went into his ritual and the supernatural took over.

"He was singing, very loud," Lorena recalls. "He had a gourd rattle that went from his hands and up to the ceiling. It was bouncing off the ceiling as he sang. I covered my eyes because I was afraid."

As the ceremony continued, Lorena heard the sound of small feet on the floor. Dexter finally spoke to her.

"He told me not to be afraid if they touched me," Lorena relates. "He said that they were doctoring me."

Lorena could then feel a sucking action against the side of her neck. She kept her hands over her eyes, more frightened than ever now. But soon it was over and the singing stopped.

When she opened her eyes the rattle was back in Dexter's hand and he was showing her the piece of toothpick that had been in her throat. She examined it and saw it was covered with a layer of white slime, the body's defense organisms against infection. The medicine man then coated her neck with white clay, said some prayers, and went on his way.

"I wish he were alive today," Lorena says. "He was such a good man and we all miss him."

Lorena Walks believes that the wonders and powers that exist around mankind in daily life are to be revered and used with respect. The powers are a gift from the Creator to help us on our way to meet Him.

There are other medicine men, and likely medicine women, among the Crow today who can make use of the medicine given their tribe by the Little People. It is not known whether this power is reserved for only certain clans or whether the medicine is for the entire Crow nation. But those who have seen and felt the power are certain it exists.

For many years people outside of the intermountain Indian tribes thought that the stories of the Little People were similar to the various legends and tales of dwarfs and elves that are an integral part of European culture, as well as other cultures. But in 1934 something happened that changed that view—and the mystery continues to this day.

It began with two men who—the stories vary in detail—were either prospecting for gold or some other mineral, or were just out exploring. They were in the Pedro Mountains just west and south of Casper, Wyoming. It is said they either blasted or somehow forced their way into a small cave and, at the back of the cave on a small ledge, discovered what appeared to be a small mummy.

The little person was sitting cross-legged, with his arms folded across his chest. His skin was leathery and it was obvious he had a set of large canine teeth. He was just seven inches high in the seated position and couldn't have stood over fourteen or sixteen inches in life. It was a find that both frightened and intrigued the two men.

They took the mummy back to Casper, where it stirred up an incredible amount of interest and press coverage. Speculation was rife as to whether or not this find substantiated the legend of the Little People in the mountains. Many believed that it did, but there were many skeptics as well.

In the early 1940s the small mummy ended up in the hands of Ivan Goodman, who paid a great deal of money for it and displayed it in a jar at his used-car dealership. He received numerous requests from scientists to allow them to examine the mummy. Goodman finally consented and began making numerous trips to New York and Chicago, where the mummy was examined in detail by anthropologists and scientists of varying backgrounds.

The controversy grew to epidemic proportions and it was soon obvious that no two scientists were going to agree on what the mummy was and how it had gotten into a remote cave in the middle of a Wyoming mountain range. Obvious to all from X rays was that the mummy indeed had human form; its skeletal structure was similar to that of the human race, varying to some degree in the regions of the wrists and eye sockets.

Some scientists strongly suggested that the mummy was merely an infant who had suffered from anencephaly and had died soon after birth. A number of others did not agree. The hair—both head and pubic—was human, and the bones, with the few exceptions, were those of a human. The development of the bones suggested that the little man must have been more than sixty years old when he died. This was determined by close examination of the epiphyseal lines in the bones, which calcify at the end of adolescence in humans. There were no epiphyseal lines present. In addition, the calcification present in the teeth and in the bones suggested a long span of years beyond birth and adolescence.

It was learned that other parts of mummies were discovered over the years in the intermountain regions of Wyoming and Montana. Whole skulls and pieces of skulls were discovered. It was said that a game warden found a whole cave filled with mummies, but was so frightened that he left immediately and never went near it again. His story came out only after the discovery of the single mummy and its subsequent media coverage.

The game warden story was focused in a remote area called Pathfinder, a basin that is now underwater. The basin was off-limits to the Indians in the region, who said the area had strong medicine and belonged to the Little People. There are a number of caves and canyons in the area, many of them now underwater.

Ivan Goodman continued his quest to answer questions until he became fatally ill during a trip to New York. He returned to Wyoming to die, and left the mummy in the hands of a museum curator, who never returned it. It is still not clear what actually happened to Ivan Goodman or to the mummy.

The mystery of the Little People has indeed not ended. In Montana and Wyoming particularly, there are a number of people who are looking for the mummy and others like the original.

In time it might be proved that a race of small people did indeed inhabit the Rocky Mountains, and that they somehow were either exterminated by enemies or became extinct in some other fashion. But nothing will verify who brings the medicine to the Crow Indians.

To the Crow and the other Indian peoples who know of the Little People, physical evidence is needed only by those who have to see, touch, or otherwise sense their surroundings on one plane of existence. The Crow Indians know that the Little People always have and always will affect their lives. The Medicine Rock will continue to receive offerings, and there will always be Crow leaders and medicine men who know the power of the Little People.

18

Secrets of
the Desert

Papago Indian Reservation
Southwestern Arizona

One man who knows the Papagos and their customs is retired archaeologist Julian Hayden. Hayden lived and worked among the Papagos, at various times, for more than half a century. More than one of their stories of life and its link to spiritualism developed while Hayden was among them, including the mysterious appearance of a Silver King pigeon in the ruins deep in Ventana Cave.

Ventana Cave is the home of whirlwind, the dust devil of Papago belief, and is the site of a perennial spring. It also contains more than twelve thousand years of human history.

Among the workers excavating the site with Hayden was a Papago named Juan Xavier. As foreman, Xavier coordinated the work and organized much of the digging. A medicine man among his people, he lived below the cave with a couple of other men.

During the excavating, Xavier would take leave on occasion to visit one of his daughters, who was dying of tuberculosis. She was being cared for in an Indian hospital near Gila Crossing and was not expected to live. Still, Xavier did not give up hope and was faithful in seeing his daughter whenever he could.

On one occasion, Xavier found renewed hope that his daughter might recover. Together with a son, he journeyed to see her and found her somewhat stronger than at any time in the recent past. She looked more radiant, with her face made up and her hair dressed for her father's visit. Xavier returned to the mine feeling better than he had for some time.

At noon the following day, the mine workers looked up and saw that a bird had flown down into the dark recesses of the cave. The bird, a Silver King pigeon, alighted among the men. It appeared unusually tame, and they assumed it was a messenger pigeon that had arrived with a message. But no message was attached to the bird's feet.

All that afternoon and throughout the next morning the pigeon remained among the men, flitting from one perch to another. They tried to catch the bird, but it remained just out of reach, always within a few feet of someone, but never close enough to touch.

Just after noon that day, a messenger came to the cave and asked for Juan Xavier. Hayden took the message, as Xavier was in the mine working. The news was that Xavier's daughter had died the previous day, just before noon.

It seemed to Hayden that Xavier was waiting for him when he called him aside and reported the news of his daughter's death. Xavier showed no emotion whatsoever, but called to his son. The two of them then departed.

A few noticed that the Silver King pigeon was no longer among the men. No sign was left behind, not even a feather.

After work was finished that evening, Hayden drove back to his headquarters in Santa Rosa with Antonio, Juan's older cousin. Hayden expressed concern to Antonio that Xavier had not seemed the least bit surprised or distressed to learn that his daughter had passed away—especially since he had been in such good spirits the previous day when he and his son had returned from the hospital.

"No, Juan was not surprised," Antonio said. He was solemn. "For you see, the pigeon was his daughter. She had come to the cave to say good-bye to her father."

The years Julian Hayden has spent as an archaeologist in the desert have left him with many memories of things good and bad—many unexplained. Among his fondest memories are those of the wildlife he observed while working. He understood why the Indian tribes of the region could communicate so well with the animals and thus learn to receive medicine from them.

As Hayden describes in Volume 29, Number 2, of the *Journal of the Southwest,* he was able to learn many of the secrets of life in the vast, open desert country that demands so much of its inhabitants.

Hayden remembers walking the southern border of the Cerro Colorado playa early one morning. The area was vegetated with dense stands of arrowweed and mesquite, and was home to coyotes and red-tailed hawks. Hayden came to a cross-trail. A coyote had been watching his approach and remained in a sitting position, its tongue hanging out, curious. Hayden passed within five feet of the coyote and said "Good morning" in Spanish, and the coyote remained seated and watched him pass.

The coyote symbolizes many things to the peoples of the desert Southwest. Hayden recalled the time he was driving a pickup filled with Papago workmen to the Ventana Cave, when a coyote, eyeing some cattle across the road, trotted into

the side of the truck and knocked itself unconscious. The
coyote lay still for a short time and then got up and wobbled
off into the desert.

At first it amused the Papagos. But then their amusement
turned into a still and solemn mood of depression. Hayden
learned later that when a coyote acts strangely, death is bound
to come to a healthy person in the village. That evening Hayden and the Papago workers learned that one of their people
had died of a stroke earlier in the day.

Coyotes hold a special place among both the Pimas and
the Papagos. Hayden remembers how coyote populations
would build up without any interference from the people, no
matter how many chickens and other fowl were taken. The
reason the coyotes are left alone goes back many years.

The majority of the Pimas and Papagos are descended
from tribes that entered the region and drove out the original
prehistoric occupants, the Hohokam, whose sacred animal was
the coyote. As a medicine animal, the coyote was revered and
was not to be disturbed. The Pimas and Papagos believe that
harming coyotes might bring bad luck, or a visit from the
spirits of the slain Hohokam from long ago.

Not far from where Hayden had passed the coyote at the
cross-trails, he was joined by two antelope, which walked just
ahead of him for nearly half a mile before breaking off up a
hill. The trail was providing Hayden with the usual fare of interesting encounters. In addition to meeting the coyote and
antelope, Hayden soon found himself in the middle of one of
nature's symbiotic hunting relationships.

A red-tailed hawk perched on a saguaro cactus just up the
trail. Nearby was a young badger with his nose to the ground,
intent on finding rodents. Hayden was downwind and the
badger didn't see him until it had almost walked up onto his
hiking boots.

"Mano," Hayden said to the badger, "don't you think you should be somewhere else?"

The startled badger curled its lips and hissed before turning away and wandering off toward a mound of earth that was its den. The hawk took flight then and Hayden knew there was a hint of disgust in the way the bird soared out into the wind. The badger will usually unearth a nest of rodents, and the rodents it misses will come out when the badger leaves. It is then that the hawk will swoop down and snatch one of them. On this day, Hayden had spoiled the hunt. It is well known that coyotes follow badgers for the same reason.

Rodents pose a nuisance to those who reside in the desert. Hayden tells of an old prospector named Juan Hernandez who was watchman for an inoperative cinder mine in the Sierra Pinnicate. The old prospector lived in a partially subterranean hut dug some three feet into the loess and cobbles and covered with a roof made of cardboard, tin, and brush.

Hernandez spoke the language of the birds and animals of the desert, and for this reason kept himself removed from people. Many were afraid of him and others accused him of witchcraft and wanted to do him harm.

Hayden tells of the time Hernandez was having trouble with mice and asked the roadrunner to help him. The roadrunner—the funny bird with the long tail that speeds down roads and trails—is known to everyone and is the symbol of the desert Southwest. The roadrunner's speed is a practical ability it uses to catch snakes and rodents. Hernandez, like most who know desert wildlife, sought to use this to his advantage.

He first took his dog aside and told him there was going to be a roadrunner sharing their hut until the mice were either eaten or driven out. The dog seemed to understand, and within a few days a roadrunner came within a short distance

of the hut. Hernandez called the bird in. After telling the bird
of his problem with the mice, and assuring it that the dog was
harmless, he got the roadrunner to indeed take up residence,
and the mice were gone within three or four days. This happened more than once, and each time Hernandez would thank
the roadrunner as he left and bid him be careful in the desert.

As there is life in the desert, so there is death—and the life
after. Hayden has experienced the other side more than once.
The one thing he has learned in all his years in the desert is
that the powers that rule this world and the universe beyond
are far more complicated than anyone can imagine; and if
these powers work at times in your behalf, it is good and the
Creator is to be thanked.

In the 1960s Hayden was working on the Pinnicate with
a gale blowing. Sand soon filled in the tracks he had followed
into where he was working. He would have to wait for the
storm to pass before he could go back out, and he wondered
how he would be able to follow the trail.

Hayden finally saw the end of the storm. The winds died
down around midnight and he began his journey out. As he
drove slowly through McDougal Pass, he tried to determine
where the road should be. Everything was a smooth sea of
sand, traced in every direction by snake tracks. The tracks were
of all sizes and shapes, made by tiny sidewinders and big
sidewinders—with their distinctive loops—as well as by large
diamondbacks and small, thin racers of various kinds. Then he
saw tracks of a different variety—human tracks that suddenly
appeared from nowhere.

Hayden got out of his vehicle and studied them. They
seemed to belong to a small child wearing shoes of some kind.
They were fresh and led north along the sand-filled road.

He got back into his vehicle and followed the small tracks
through the maze of snake marks. Suddenly he couldn't see

them anymore. Once again he got out to look. They had vanished.

Hayden looked down the hill and saw the ranch he remembered passing while coming in to work. He had found his way out by following the tracks of the small child. When he reached the ranch he asked if anyone had come through since he had. He was told few people ever went up into the high Pinnicate past the ranch, since the sandstorms make it hard to find the way out. No, no one at all had come through. No adults, no children. No one but himself.

After thinking about it for some time, Hayden decided there would never be an explanation for the footprints. It was sufficient to realize they had appeared and to let it go at that.

Julian Hayden is now retired, but he still gets out into his beloved desert country to walk the hills and playas. He doesn't walk as far or as long as he once did, but just being there is enough to warm his soul. Seeing the desert and knowing something, even a little, of its vast mysteries is more than enough to keep the spirit high and the senses asking for more.

Though it is harsh and at times appears barren to the untrained eye, the desert is the essence of life. It is a place where every drop of water is used efficiently and where the slightest change in temperature means new life. It has a spirit of its own and it is vast—but it is never empty.

19

The Face of
the Wolf

Dulce, New Mexico
Jicarilla Apache Indian Reservation

Among the Apache Indians there exist spiritual leaders whose lives are dedicated to the physical and mental growth of their people. They learn to use special gifts given to them by the Creator to teach their young people the Sacred Way. These men are rare and their lives are given to helping and healing others in ways they themselves do not always understand, but certainly respect. They have powers that can appear over-whelming to the imagination.

One such man has learned the powers, and says that he will never learn all there is to know, that no one can. This man is named Morgan, and the Chiricahua Apache—living on the Jicarilla Reservation—are his people. He is as closely linked to the heritage of these Apache as any living man can be, for he has the medicine of one of their greatest leaders. He is a great-great-grandson of Geronimo.

As with any medicine man, Morgan is able to bring a new

approach to life to those who believe in the power of the Sacred Way. His knowledge has been gained through acceptance of the powers that exist, and he acknowledges that the chosen can perform remarkable feats—including tapping deep into the powers of the supernatural.

"This is something accepted by our people," Morgan says. "We don't question, we accept."

Morgan and others like him work to bring the power of truth to those who wish to learn it. They do not restrict themselves to any race of people, but consider everyone a brother under the Creator. The fight to promote this truth is an everlasting one and can at times be overwhelming.

Morgan tells of Whistle-fire, an elder among the Chiricahua people who once faced the challenge of protecting the Sacred Way. He was a medicine man with incredible faith and power. Among his people he was known as a shape-shifter. His medicine was so strong he could transform himself into a wolf. Whistle-fire knew the meaning of this power and how it was to be used.

"The Apache people know that the more a person understands the Sacred Way, the harder it is for them to live in this world," Morgan says. "Whistle-fire was especially aware of this and found it to be a considerable challenge in working with the young people. He found it difficult to make the old values seem that important to the younger Apache, for their lives are often centered around the material things that overwhelm the modern world."

Morgan himself knows the difficulties of teaching, but he remains persistent; those who teach will not be defeated. Anyone who interferes with the teachings of the Apache people to their young can find themselves literally looking into the face of the wolf.

As Morgan witnessed it, the wolf came to demand justice for the Apache people in the spring of 1984. One man in-

volved was a white sheriff named Kestler who ran his county
with an iron hand, but did not recognize where his authority
ended and the civil rights of others began. Another was a minister who had his mind set on driving something he considered
evil from the minds of his followers, even if it meant stepping
onto sacred Apache lands to do it. And it dealt with two young
Apache boys who had gone hunting together, only to become
the victims of the minister and the sheriff—until Whistle-fire,
who was grandfather to one of the boys, taught the two men
that the meaning of life was not to control others.

Michael and Thomas had known each other from the time
they could walk and ride a horse. They rode often together
around their village and sneaked up to steal fry bread from the
women. Their bond was strong and developing into the kind
of closeness that only warriors know.

"Spring is a traditional time to go out from the villages to
hunt," Morgan says. "This particular spring the boys, who were
approaching manhood, were to begin their search for their individual powers. That they were to go together would give
them additional power."

Michael told his grandfather about the upcoming hunt.
Whistle-fire was proud that his grandson had been invited to
hunt with the son of another leader. This meant the two boys
would begin their quest for the meaning of life and the power
that comes with it. The boys would be alone on a sacred
mountain to learn the old ways, when men went out to hunt
and became bonded as brothers. Nothing could have pleased
Whistle-fire more.

The fathers of Michael and Thomas celebrated in their
own way, renewing the bonds between warriors of the Apache
nation. Their sons were going up to the sacred mountain to
gain power and thus bring honor to their families.

When their mothers had prepared their things, the boys

met with their fathers and then set off for the sacred mountain. Michael and Thomas both understood the significance of what they were doing and were anxious to begin the quest toward manhood. They would be able to come back and look into the eyes of all the other young men with confidence. The older young men who had gone before would now respect them. And their fathers would watch with pride.

Michael and Thomas went about their hunt with the respect expected of them. They opened their senses to the things around them and saw that the land was strong and could teach them much about life. This was a sacred time for them and they knew they would forever carry the memory of this hunt.

Things were good on the mountain and the air was fresh and clean, with the strength of nature all around. The water sang over the rocks, and the drooping boughs of the Palo Verde were green and heavy with leaves. Birds talked to the two boys as they climbed higher onto the mountain, praying to the game they might find, hoping the soul of the animal would forgive them for bringing it death.

"But someone else saw them going up onto the mountain," Morgan recalls. "There was a new minister who had moved in to try to change the minds of the Apache people and have them learn his way of teaching. He was having a hard time convincing the people his way was right, and he had decided if he could break up some of the traditional steps to manhood practiced by the Apache, he could succeed in gaining control over them.

"What the minister did not understand about the Apache people was that they knew him better than he knew himself. They could see that this minister did not really believe in the religion he was teaching but was simply hiding behind it to gain power and control. The Apache people know that to have true power, you must be true to yourself and the Creator."

The lives of the Apache are dedicated to truth, and this minister did not represent that. He considered the Apache to be stubborn and ignorant; they needed to be taught a lesson. When he saw the two boys going up onto the mountain, he thought this would be a good time to begin his efforts to gain control of the people.

The minister called the sheriff and told him that two young Apache boys were hunting together on this mountain, no doubt doing something against the law. The sheriff agreed, saying it was important that the Apache realize they had to live by the codes imposed on all other people in New Mexico. They had to accept God in the same way the white man did. Why did these Indians think they could go back to their traditional ways? That had to be stopped. The two boys had to be doing something wrong up there, and if it wasn't obvious, there sure was something that could be trumped up. That would be no problem.

The sheriff took some deputies along and went with the minister to where the boys were sleeping. The sheriff pulled the blanket from the two boys, and the deputies began beating them, while the minister stood to one side and smiled. This was the only way these people would learn who was in charge, and then he could make some progress in converting them.

"They beat the boys up pretty bad," Morgan recalls. "They really stomped them, just two boys who didn't know why it was happening."

Nearly unconscious, Michael and Thomas were hauled to jail. They were thrown into a cell and left there. The minister felt that he now had them filled with fear and that he could tell them what he wanted them to hear and make them believe it. He grew angry when he thought he had come so far to this reservation only to have the Apache disregard his teachings.

The minister began his well-rehearsed sermon, which he

used in his own culture. He told the boys that he was the only one they should ever listen to for direction. He told them over and over that it had been wrong for them to go hunting together on the sacred mountain, to learn the accepted Indian way, the Sacred Way, to achieve spiritual power. The only way to learn was through him, the minister said. He warned them again and told them to tell their friends that the same thing would happen to anyone else who went up there.

The minister urged them to ignore the teachings of Whistle-fire, who had often been accused of practicing witchcraft by those who didn't understand. The minister said his way was the accepted way now, not the old ways that had brought their people into bondage more than a century before.

Michael and Thomas's fathers went to the jail, but neither could get his son released.

"They were told to leave or be thrown into a cell themselves," Morgan recalls. "It didn't seem to them that there had been any reason to do this to Michael and Thomas. More importantly, they wanted to get the boys out before the old medicine man, Whistle-fire, heard of this injustice."

Michael's father spent considerable time trying to get the sheriff to understand that the Apache way was strong, and that interfering in something that was sacred, let alone beating the boys as well, was something that would make the old medicine man extremely angry.

"Michael's father told the sheriff that it was important he release the two boys," Morgan says. "But the sheriff told them it was more important that they get the hell out of there if they didn't want to receive the same. Michael's father worried that the sheriff would meet with tragedy unless he listened to reason."

But the sheriff was getting pressure from the minister, who constantly worked on him, telling him the boys had to suffer for what they had done. He knew the sheriff needed little convincing—he enjoyed beating people—but the minister wanted to gain psychological control of the sheriff as well.

Michael and Thomas continued to be held in jail. They were given little to eat and by the next night had grown quite weak. Michael's father finally decided to contact a friend.

"That's when I got the call," Morgan says. "I knew the old shape-shifter, Whistle-fire, and knew what would happen if the old medicine man grew angry with the sheriff and the minister. Those two men had no idea what they were in for."

By the time Morgan had reached the reservation, Whistle-fire had already heard what had happened to Michael and Thomas. He was on his way to the jail.

"The sheriff hit the old man and told him he wasn't afraid of any witchcraft," Morgan says. "Whistle-fire left without saying anything, and then I tried to warn the sheriff myself. He told me the same thing—that he wasn't afraid of anything. Then I told him he had better be careful, and he had better have concern for his family."

Later that night the sheriff got a phone call from his wife, who was in hysterics. She told him they had been watching television when a wolf had jumped through the bedroom window and held her and the two children hostage for a time before finally leaving. She could hardly speak, she was so terrified, and she was afraid the wolf would return.

The sheriff grabbed one of his favorite rifles and sped home to his family. He couldn't imagine that what Morgan had just warned him of was actually coming to pass, that the old medicine man was using his powers. To the sheriff it didn't matter, for he was confident that the wolf would be no match for the rifle.

But the sheriff didn't even have a chance to raise his rifle. When he got out of the patrol car, an enormous black shape lunged out of the night and knocked him to the ground. It was a wolf, but its growl was half like that of a man's yelling.

"That wolf tore big chunks of flesh out of the sheriff's arms and shoulders," Morgan recalls. "The sheriff might have died, but the wolf was only teaching him a lesson—giving him a second chance. You had better bet that sheriff ordered those two boys released immediately, and he became a believer."

The minister became a believer as well. Holding a cross in front of him, he met the huge wolf at his door. Such a defense is only as good as the person's faith in it; the minister's faith must have been sorely lacking.

"That minister got a shock he never recovered from," Morgan relates. "The wolf stood up on its hind legs and immediately changed into the form of a man. The man grabbed the cross from the minister's hands and laid it on a table. Then the man changed back into a wolf and dropped back down on all fours, while the minister lost consciousness."

When his arms and shoulders had healed as much as they ever would, the sheriff resumed his duties a changed man. The minister left the area and no replacement was ever sent. The sacred mountain had been protected and the Apache way of life restored by one of the peoples' strongest powers.

According to Morgan, such powers are used only when they are deemed necessary, and when the Sacred Way is violated in the terrible way it was with Michael and Thomas. Morgan himself practices as a medicine man and travels the United States and the world teaching those who seek him out to heal their old scars and begin fresh new lives—to find themselves and enjoy, for once, a total and whole existence.

There are a lot of truths to be learned from the old ways, when the world revolved at a slower pace and people interacted with one another on a more spiritual level. It was a time when people could become close to one another and share their lives in a more compassionate way. It is a way that is coming back to the Apache people, as well as to other peoples of other races. And those on the Jicarilla Apache Reservation can be assured that the wolf will walk down the path of truth forever.

20

The
Snake People

The Place of the Pit
The Central Rocky Mountain Region

Among Native American people, there exists a realm of horror that affects their daily lives. They seem to be aware of constricting influences that seep from the darkness and grip their souls. They are caught fast in it and must live with their nightmares.

Because of this, they are able to see and feel presences so abominable that even the strongest of their people cannot deal with them. The only way to handle the evils is to avoid them whenever possible or to appease them whenever they make demands. The more demands they make, the deeper the despair.

The Snake People have always brought fear to Native Americans. They are an entity that cannot be dealt with, and they belong to no tribe other than their own, having their own culture and customs—and they certainly are not to be confused with the Shoshone people, who are often referred to historically as the Snake Indians; or the Zuni tribe, who conduct ceremonies with snakes to ensure successful crops and other blessings on their people.

The Snake People are their own kind and, like their name, they live the way of the viper. They are a people to be left alone entirely. To know of them is one thing, but to disturb them can end anyone's earthly days.

Those who know much about the Snake People have witnessed things that no one could ever believe. But one man says such things do happen. He will be called Mahlan here, and he is Apache. Mahlan is himself a man of power and knows that to challenge intense evil is to bring a world of hell into your own mind. If evil attacks, Mahlan knows how to shield against it. But he says it is a grave mistake to take on dark powers that cannot be conquered. There is little that Mahlan fears, but he will not arouse the anger of the Snake People.

Mahlan learned of the Snake People as a child from his people. He knew they existed and that they were of a dark world. He knew to avoid them and never to challenge them in any way. But on a summer night in 1982, Mahlan learned by accident why the Snake People are forced to live as they do.

Mahlan will never forget the night he traveled to a place deep in the mountains to visit his sister, who was married to a white rancher there. When he reached the high country, the sun had already set. Darkness can play tricks on the mind, especially when fear is in control. But Mahlan grew up in the Indian way and accepted that the supernatural does exist.

"I became very alarmed at what happened to me that night," Mahlan says. "I have seen much and have helped others overcome their fears, but this is so strong and so evil that there is nothing on this earth that can touch it."

As Mahlan remembers that night, he was not far from his

sister's house when he reached a gate near a stream and got out of his car to open it. There was something strong in the air, a clinging, musky odor that reminded Mahlan of a huge snake den. There was no mistaking the strong smell of the pit viper.

When he got back into his car, he saw something just out of reach of his headlight beams. He saw large, slitted yellow eyes, with a distance between the eyes that a man could step across. And there was something moving just in front of the eyes that Mahlan could barely make out—something that darted in and out. Something huge, with a long, flickering tongue, was watching him.

"I thought I was finished right there," Mahlan says. "I saw those eyes and the forked tongue. It seemed to me that I could not escape, that I should prepare for the end."

But the eyes finally disappeared into the night. Mahlan could hear movement, as if something heavy were dragging or slithering itself across the road. He put his car in gear and drove away as fast as he could.

When he reached the ranch, he greeted his sister and brother-in-law but did not mention the terrifying experience he had just had along the river. He ate and talked of old times, and listened while his brother-in-law talked about ranching and how it was becoming harder to make a living at it.

What struck Mahlan as more than coincidence was that his brother-in-law was losing livestock along the river. Usually they would just disappear, but at other times they would be found lying dead near the water with large puncture wounds in their back.

"I took one of those cows to a vet one time," Mahlan's brother-in-law said. "There was more than enough venom in that cow to kill two hundred head of livestock. He couldn't explain it and I never saw anyone so scared."

"You will likely be missing more cows tomorrow morning," Mahlan told him.

When Mahlan's brother-in-law asked him why he would say a thing like that, he told him there was something down by the river and that he had just seen it. He described the eyes and the smell, and the sound of something gigantic slithering down the hill. Mahlan's sister nodded and said she knew he had seen it, for he still smelled of the viper.

Perplexed, Mahlan's brother-in-law looked at his wife, then asked her what she was talking about. It had been a secret she had kept from her husband since they had moved to the ranch only a few years before. She, like Mahlan, knew of the Snake People and had agreed to offer them cattle to feed the huge snake that lived in a pit high on the mountain. That was the reason they had been missing cattle.

Mahlan listened while his sister told her husband the entire story of the Snake People and the place of the huge pit viper. She said they were a race of Indians who lived in the heavy rocks and timber above the ranch, but were also scattered through other parts of the West where they took up secret residence and held their rituals. They embraced and worshiped and bred with the snake, so that the offspring could become either man or snake at will.

"Why have you held this from me for so long?" Mahlan's brother-in-law asked his wife.

"Because it is something you do not want to believe. Even after seeing the dead cattle filled with venom and knowing that a hundred snakes did not attack them, you chose to simply say they had died and nothing else. This evil is something we must live with, and it can only be done through sacrifice."

Mahlan's sister went on to tell more about the enormous pit viper, a rattlesnake, that resides in a deep den in the mountains near the ranch. The serpent has been there as long as anyone can remember, and it is imperative that it be appeased, or it will turn loose its powers against the Snake People and all of the world.

"They offer a sacrifice to it," Mahlan's sister said. "The first-born male baby of the Snake People is offered to the serpent each spring. I saw it once and I'll never go back."

Mahlan's sister said she had been forced to witness the sacrifice in order to seal the agreement between her and the Snake People, so that she and her husband could keep their ranch and not be harmed by the serpent. As she described the ritual, the baby is placed on a platform and lowered deep into the pit. The baby soon senses what is about to happen and begins to scream in such a way that the sound never leaves those who hear it—the most ghastly sound of fear and terror that could ever be imagined. Then there is a sound like a thousand heavy rattles being shaken all at once, which drowns out the screaming. Suddenly both the screaming and the rattling stop, and the platform is brought back to the surface—always empty.

"The government learned about all this," Mahlan's sister said. "Since the pit was on government land, they decided to investigate. They hired two archaeologists and told them to gather what information they could. These archaeologists found the pit and decided they wanted to go down into it. They had been warned. But you know how the government is—they won't listen to anything."

The two archaeologists were lowered into the pit with ropes, while other government officials waited for them. They kept in touch with the men with two-way radios. Deep in the den the men tried to call back up, to have themselves pulled out, but the radios wouldn't work.

The heavy rattling began, followed by the screams of the men. When the ropes were hauled up, one of the men was

missing and the other was dead. He had suffered some kind of
wound to the middle of his body that had completely dissolved his stomach and lower chest. It was determined that the
oozing material around the huge opening was composed of
pure protein.

"The government had somebody go up there with a big
bulldozer and push a giant rock on top of that pit," Mahlan's
sister said. "They thought they could seal it off and solve the
problem. But two nights later the rock had been moved and
the pit was open again. No one wants to admit how the rock
was moved; no one wants to believe in the horror. But it is
there."

Mahlan's brother-in-law looked at him and said, "None of
this is true."

Mahlan shrugged. "I know what I saw. Not everybody
sees the same things, but I know what I saw."

"And I know what I saw," Mahlan's sister added.

The next morning Mahlan took his brother-in-law to
where he had opened the gate the night before and had seen
the huge slitted eyes watching him. Mahlan pointed to a place
in the middle of the road where it appeared a huge form of
some kind had slithered over the tracks of Mahlan's car.

"Now do you believe?" Mahlan asked.

Mahlan's brother-in-law then looked at him and said em-
phatically, "I see what you're saying, but tell me, can you always
believe what your eyes are showing you? Can you always
count on what your senses are bringing to you when you're
clouded with fear? I'm going to have to let my gut feeling set-
tle this one later."

Mahlan's brother-in-law walked away, and Mahlan just
shrugged. He watched his brother-in-law drive back up
toward the ranch. He got into his car and turned it down the
mountain. He would be back up to see his sister again, and he
knew that when he arrived the huge serpent would be watch-

ing him. He knew also that his brother-in-law was living right next to it and refused to acknowledge its existence. Perhaps that was best, Mahlan thought. If it wasn't bothering you inside your head, you weren't apt to see it. But if it had already managed to crawl deep into your mind, there was no getting rid of it.

21

The Face

Upper Missouri River
Northeastern Montana

Poplar, Montana, the agency headquarters for the Fort Peck Indian Reservation, sits on the banks of the Missouri River. The town was established in 1880, and many old buildings are still left, each with stories from the past.

The Assiniboine-Sioux people all know the Head Start building, where the first Indian health service was located. Marise Headdress, who was ten years old in the autumn of 1986, remembers spending the most terrifying moments of her life there.

It was a cool evening in early November. Nightfall was coming and Marise had just arrived at Head Start from school. She had intended to meet her grandmother, Bobbi Clincher, and get a ride home.

A lot of things would happen, however, before Marise ever got to see her grandmother.

It was four-thirty in the afternoon. The teachers and office staff were leaving the building. Marise learned that her grandmother had driven to Wolf Point on business and would return shortly.

Marise decided to wait in her grandmother's office, in the basement at the foot of the stairs. She took her schoolbag and made herself comfortable.

Verna Grey Bull, one of the coordinators, tried to talk her out of staying, offering to give her a ride home. Marise thanked her, but wanted to wait for her grandmother.

"I'll leave the lights on in the hall," Verna said. "Someone else might still be here."

After Verna Grey Bull had left, Marise turned off the hall lights. They weren't needed. There was no one left in the building. At least that's what she believed.

The sun had fallen and Marise was alone, looking at magazines in her grandmother's office, when strange things began to happen.

"I kept hearing footsteps on the stairs," Marise remembers. "And toilets flushing. At first I thought it was the cleaning people. Then I remembered, they hadn't come yet."

The noises soon included banging, like someone hitting pipes in the ceiling above Marise's head. It seemed at times that the pipes might break and fall on her.

Marise had heard her grandmother talk about ghosts in the building, but she hadn't really believed it. Now she felt differently; she *had* to be hearing ghosts.

"I told them to knock it off," Marise says. "My gramma would say that if she yelled at them, they would be quiet for a while. With me, they just kept up the noise. I got scared."

Marise decided to leave. She picked up her schoolbag and turned the light off. She stepped into the hall and felt very strange.

"The air was thick and kind of cloudy," Marise says. "It smelled a little like cigar smoke."

Then she noticed a dim light coming from a classroom at the end of the hall.

"I knew that I had turned all the lights off," Marise recalls. "I started down the hall, thinking maybe I had missed one somehow. The air seemed more and more hazy. Everything felt very strange."

As Marise got closer to the room, she realized something was very wrong.

"It was the classroom for three-year-olds. There was a big window near the door that the teacher kept covered with black construction paper, so that the students wouldn't be distracted by people walking past the room. I couldn't understand it. The paper was off the window and a dim light was showing through."

Marise saw a man suddenly appear in the window. He was old and wrinkled, with long, scraggly white hair. He was facing sideways, as though he was sitting down.

"I stopped because I didn't know who he was," Marise says. "His skin was pasty, and his hair stuck out everywhere. I didn't know what he was doing there."

Then the man's head turned.

"When he looked at me, I couldn't move," Marise remembers. "His eyes were sunken in. They were strange and piercing, like he was staring right through me. And his lips were cracked all over. His face kept getting bigger, like it was moving toward me."

Marise turned and ran. She rushed up the stairs and pushed through the door, gasping for breath. She crossed the playground, dazed and confused, looking back at the building as she ran.

Marise remembers how scared she was. "I guess I didn't

know what to do. I was confused. I couldn't understand what had happened, or why. I found myself next to the Catholic church. Verna Grey Bull was driving by and she stopped to pick me up.

"She asked me what had happened. I told her that I had gotten scared in the building. I said nothing about the old man in the window. Verna just nodded."

Marise decided to go to her mother's house to wait for her grandmother. Verna drove her there, wondering what had happened. Still, Marise said nothing about the old man.

Later, Marise's grandmother picked her up and they started for home. On the way, they turned toward the Head Start building.

"I asked Gramma where we were going," Marise recalls. "I was afraid and didn't want to go back. Gramma said it was important that she pick up some papers. I didn't want to stay out in the car, so I went inside with her."

Marise didn't want to go into the basement, but wouldn't tell her grandmother why. Finally, Marise decided she would go. When she looked down the hall, she became doubly confused.

There was no haze or smoke in the hallway. The construction paper was over the window, just as it was supposed to be, and the lights were all off.

"I began to doubt what I had seen," Marise says. "I thought maybe none of it had been real. But deep inside of me, I knew it had been real. I was still very scared."

Marise finally calmed down a bit and began to ask her grandmother questions.

"I wanted to know all about the classroom at the end of the hall," Marise says. "Gramma wanted to go down there, but I didn't. I asked her who the old man was, and if he had been one of the cleaning people. She asked me what he looked like and I told her. We didn't go down to the class-room. Instead, my grandmother quickly got the things she had come for, and we left."

On the way home, Marise's grandmother turned down the street that led to the hospital. Marise thought she was just getting more papers for work. But inside the hospital, a strange thing happened.

Marise noticed a large picture hanging on the wall of the waiting room. It was of an old man with white, scraggly hair, whose eyes were strange and piercing.

"That's him! That's the man I saw!" Marise told her grand-mother. "Who is he?"

Marise's grandmother explained that it was a picture of a doctor who had once lived in the community.

"She told me that his name was Doc Swanson," Marise says. "She told me that he had smoked cigars, and that he had died many years before. I had seen his ghost."

Doc Swanson, as he was affectionately known, was the first chief of staff at the Poplar community hospital. When he died in the late 1960s he had served the community for more than thirty years.

During his life, Doc Swanson was very active at the Indian Health Clinic. He loved children and devoted his life to car-ing for those in need. He never married, for it is said the only woman he had ever loved turned him down. He had been many years older than she.

Doc Swanson became a near recluse, living only for his work. It would seem that he never wanted to leave the clinic, even in death.

Bobbi Clincher, Marise's grandmother, wonders whether the old doctor might still want to be in charge. She certainly has grounds for believing that.

In the summer of 1980, remodeling began in the old building to accommodate a Head Start program for Poplar's preschool children. Bobbi became education coordinator in November of that year. She worked long and hard trying to get the building in shape for classes. But it seemed as if someone wanted the project to fail.

"We couldn't keep workers on the job," Bobbi remembers. "A crew of electricians walked out. They left their tools and ladders and never came back. I think the tools are still there today."

One main problem with the remodeling was that the new plumbing pipes wouldn't stay together. Though no one but Bobbi, her husband, and the program director had keys for the building, it often appeared as if someone had gone into the basement and pulled the pipes apart.

"It occurred to me that Doc Swanson was angry about the changes," Bobbi suggests. "I finally got tired of it. We weren't bothering him, but he was making it awfully hard for us. I decided to confront the old doctor, as strange as that sounds."

Bobbi remembers the day when she stood at the bottom of the stairs near the coffee room, her back against the wall. "We're going to have this Head Start center," she told the spirit. "The children need this. You should have enough consideration for the children to leave us alone."

The tactic seemed to work. The pipes stayed together and the Head Start program got under way.

But the strange occurrences in the building continued.

"The past just wouldn't give up," Bobbi recalls. "The haze and smoke lingered in the basement, and the banging in the ceiling continued off and on. Doors would open and close by themselves, especially the big one in front. We would frequently feel the presence of someone, though we could see no one around. It was even common to hear the rustle of silk in the hallways, as if nurses were walking about in their starched uniforms."

In addition, teachers and students often heard conversations in empty rooms and footsteps in the halls when no one was there. Some reported hearing a dental drill in operation, when there hadn't been dental work done in the building for many years.

On one occasion, a teacher ran out of the building and stopped the afternoon bus. She told the driver she had seen a small boy in one of the classrooms. When she returned to get the boy, she saw him reaching for a ball. Suddenly he disappeared. She had to tell the bus driver that she had been mistaken.

Though Marise Headdress and Bobbi Clincher no longer live in Poplar, they both remember their experiences in the Head Start building. Many have had similar experiences there; anyone who lives or has ever lived in Poplar knows stories about the building.

Many believe the reason for the unrest lies in the fact that the basement was once a mortuary. Many say they can still smell death in the basement, that it will never leave.

Everyone agrees, though, that no harm has ever befallen anyone who has worked or gone to school there. Many say the old doctor is looking after the children, keeping them from harm in some fashion.

"Among Indian people," Bobbi Clincher says, "the family is a very important unit. Actually, the family extends out to aunts and uncles and grandparents on both sides. Everyone raises the children.

"Maybe the old doctor, during his many years at the health service, learned a lot from the people. Maybe the children are still part of his family and he knows nothing else. The children are a blessing to us, very important. They are very close to the Creator. Maybe, in some way, he's looking for the Creator."

So the mysterious footsteps and the thumping in the walls and ceilings continue. The smell of cigar smoke still hangs in the air, and visions of the past remain behind. Perhaps they will linger there forever.

22

Sacred Ground

**Tongue and Powder River Country
Northern Wyoming,
Southern and Eastern Montana**

As a boy and young man, John Young loved to roam the open country along the foothills of the Bighorn Mountains. The rock outcrops studded with pine and juniper hadn't changed since the days of the free-roaming Sioux and Cheyenne Indians.

"Time seemed to stand still out there," John recalls. "I would often find arrowheads and tools they had worked with many years before. The place hadn't changed in all that time."

John saw no harm in gathering an arrowhead or two, but during the summer of his sixteenth year, he learned how important it was to leave the dead alone.

"That spring there had been a lot of rain and Tongue River had flooded," John says. "I was walking along, after the water had receded, and found where a cave in the bank had been exposed. I saw something red, like cloth, among the rocks in the cave, and, curious, I crawled in to see what it was.

"What I found was a human skeleton wrapped in a blanket. It looked to me like an old Indian burial, a woman, with the nicest blue bead necklace you ever saw around her neck."

John took the necklace and closed the blanket. He didn't think twice about it. She didn't need it anymore.

Back at the family ranch, John placed the necklace in a drawer in his room. He didn't tell his parents about it for fear they would make him give it up. Within a few days, John began to wonder why he had taken it.

"Things began to really go wrong for me," he recalls. "I cut my finger chopping wood. I'd never done that before. And a horse nearly ran me over in the backyard, an old horse that could hardly break out of a walk."

What bothered John most of all were the things that started happening at night. He began having bad dreams, seeing angry faces. Then he awoke one night to see the Indian woman at the foot of his bed.

"I knew it was her, though I couldn't see her clearly. She was filmy, wrapped in the red blanket, her hair long and loose behind her. She didn't say anything. She just stared at me. I would start to yell and she would disappear. But she came back night after night."

John finally took the blue bead necklace back to the cave and placed it exactly where he had found it, around the skeleton's neck. He did the work with shaky hands.

"I thought she might rise up at any time and grab me," he remembers. "I just hurried up and got out of there fast. I never went back and I never bothered another grave. I never will."

———

It is held as a firm belief among Indian people that the spirit stays with the individual who has met death until after the bones have decayed and returned to dust. That is why burial grounds have always remained sacred to Native Americans and why they are so cautious about the dead. They would never think of disturbing a body, lest the spirit brought to unrest come to haunt them as a result.

Bill Tall Bull, a Northern Cheyenne from Busby, Montana, is a historian and an elder among the Northern Cheyenne. His Indian name is Feather Wolf, and he is the great-grandson of Morning Star (also called Dull Knife), who led the Northern Cheyenne north from Oklahoma to freedom during the winter of 1879.

Tall Bull is close to the earth and is respected for his sense of natural values. He is often called upon to speak to civic groups and organizations about the traditions of Native American culture.

He has also been taught in the old ways of medicine and religion. For this reason he is often asked to assist in the reburial of skeletal remains and to investigate sites where building and development will take place, so that any problems can be forestalled.

Tall Bull has the ability to sense if there has been any tragedy or death in the immediate area, or whether any gravesites lie nearby. These features contribute to the restlessness of an area and the hauntings that are often reported in new houses or developments.

"Many things can happen to cause problems in the ground," Tall Bull says. "Usually the disruption of a burial site will cause the most problems, if someone doesn't make the spirit rest easy once again."

In 1987, Tall Bull was called to a site in eastern Montana where a contractor was rebuilding a county road, making it into a two-lane highway. During the excavations, the crew had unearthed an ancient grave.

"It was a young girl from an old, old culture," Tall Bull recalls. "I was to rebury her and I was uneasy. For some reason I didn't think I should put her into the grave on her back, but I didn't know how to properly lay her out. I had no idea, because I knew she wasn't Cheyenne, or from any Plains tribe that I was familiar with. I just didn't know what to do with her.

"But then a spirit came from the south—white, almost clear, and with no face. This spirit instructed me so that I placed her on her side, facing west, toward the setting sun. The spirit told me that her eyes were not to have the sun cross over them, but instead to face her where the sun fell. I don't know of any people who do this. None. But that is what the spirit told me to do. So I did it."

There are elders like Bill Tall Bull within each tribe who have similar stories to tell. They come from a long tradition of reverence toward all life and a continued respect for that life after the soul has left the body.

These people used to hold their traditions very close, guarding them against outsiders. But those times are in the past and their thinking is changing.

It is now their belief that the time has come for the dissemination of ancient knowledge, so that Earth, the mother, may be more revered by our modern society. As a part of this society, Indian peoples everywhere struggle daily with a culture they cannot fully understand.

Because of this, Native American teachers are now willing to share ancient songs and dances, in hopes that all races and cultures will someday treat the land with the aim of conservation, not exploitation.

It is imperative, these Native American teachers emphasize, that Earth's children come together and revere all life as one, and thus save ourselves from certain natural disaster.

"A good beginning is to realize that life is sacred, very sacred," Bill Tall Bull says. "The dead should be considered with respect and left in peace. They are our ancestors; they are part of us."

John Young couldn't agree more.

23

Night of
the Blizzard

Pine Ridge Indian Reservation
Southwestern South Dakota

In December 1985, Alice Seidel was driving from Colorado
Springs to Bismarck, North Dakota, to spend the holidays
with relatives. Widowed for three years, she would be making
the journey by herself for the first time. She wanted to surprise
her daughter and her daughter's family.

Alice had planned her trip carefully, taking an extra day,
not wanting to push herself. But after car trouble just south of
Denver, she was running two days late.

Upon reaching Cheyenne, Wyoming, Alice filled her car's
tank with gas, bought a Nebraska map and turned east, push-
ing herself to make up the time, hoping the shortcut would
bring her into Bismarck by early Christmas Eve.

Leaving the interstate, though, was taking a grave risk during a northern winter. Alice Seidel would discover this before
her trip was through.

At Sidney, Nebraska, Alice turned north, weaving her way

across the Panhandle on small, two-lane highways. Traffic was sparse and the air was getting colder. News of an impending snowstorm came from all the radio stations. It was predicted to arrive late on Christmas Day.

Exhausted, Alice stopped in Chadron, in northern Nebraska. She was determined to get an early start the next morning. After two fitful hours of sleep, though, she returned to her car.

"There was a light snowfall beginning," she remembers. "I knew that the storm was coming in earlier than they had predicted. I thought I could cross South Dakota before the storm hit. I didn't care that it was the dead of night; I wanted to beat it. I was determined to make it to my daughter's. I guess I wasn't thinking of my own safety."

The wind and snowfall increased, making visibility poor. By the time she had reached the Pine Ridge Indian Reservation, the snow was flying in blinding sheets.

"I didn't have any idea where I was," Alice said later. "I stopped to look at the map a number of times, but I couldn't make heads or tails of it. I took a turn north when I should have stayed on a road leading east."

Alice's car began to act up, coughing and sputtering. She remembered something about the fuel pump. She thought it had been replaced. To add to her troubles, the car was sliding on the slick pavement, narrowly missing going into the ditch.

"Finally the engine quit," Alice remembers. "I was stranded in a sea of snow. I was sure I was going to die. That's when I saw the three Indians. They were dressed in rags and looked almost like skeletons."

Alice was more afraid of the men than she was of the weather. They walked up from the ditch and stood in her headlights. One of them came to the window. Alice remembers rolling down the window slightly and looking into his face.

"He was hard to see because of the darkness and the snow.

But I suddenly wasn't afraid anymore. He asked me if I had trouble, and said that he would look at the engine. He spoke in broken English. I asked him why they were out in the storm and he told me they had seen my headlights. They wanted to help."

Alice released the latch on the hood and the three worked for a short time. Finally, the same Indian came to her window again and told her to start her car. To her delight, the engine ran smoothly.

"The Indian told me to go back down to the intersection where I had turned north. He said to turn left, that I would see the sun coming up in the east. He told me that the storm had nearly passed."

Alice asked whether she could pay them for their trouble, but the Indian had turned from her window and all three were walking off into the storm.

"I wanted to offer them a ride somewhere since they had been so good to me," Alice recalls. "But they were gone. Just gone."

After turning her car around, Alice drove to the intersection and turned left. Relieved, she headed her car into a light that was breaking in the east, making driving much easier.

Some sixty miles farther, Alice stopped in the small town of Martin, at a diner just opening for breakfast. A startled waitress asked her how she had made it through the storm.

"She wondered how I could even see," Alice remembers. "I told her about my car trouble and the three men who had helped me and had given me direction."

Alice explained that one of the men had instructed her to just keep driving east, toward the rising sun. She recalls the waitress's reaction.

"She just stared at me. She wanted to know where the men had helped me. I told her and she said I had been near Wounded Knee. I remember that she pointed out a window and said, 'Look, the sun is just now rising. You couldn't have driven all that way in so short a time."

Confused, Alice looked at her watch for the first time since the ordeal had begun. It was barely eight A.M.

Alice finished her breakfast and went on, wondering what had happened. She now realized the men couldn't have just been Indians living near the road. Something had told her that at the time. But who had they been?

She kept telling herself they couldn't be ghosts.

"I had seen some things as a child," Alice says. "I remembered seeing my grandfather after he died. He had come into my room. But as an adult, I hadn't thought about those things much."

Not being a student of history, Alice had no knowledge of the Battle of Wounded Knee, just after Christmas in 1890, during which a number of Sioux Indians had been killed by U.S. Cavalry soldiers. She only knew that she was grateful to the three men, whoever they were, who had helped her and had saved her life.

Alice Seidel arrived at her surprised daughter's house early on Christmas Eve, tired but happy. Later that evening, Alice was to receive a surprise of her own, in the form of an older sister she hadn't seen in many years.

"We had had a parting of the ways when she had married a man I didn't like," Alice says. "She had kept in touch with my daughter, who always said we'd come together again some day. I had always felt bad about it. After all, it was her life. I shouldn't have interfered."

Alice learned that her sister's husband had suffered a fatal heart attack the month before. The sister had driven out from Michigan to her niece's home for Christmas, in hopes of learning where Alice was living and maybe reconciling.

"We talked all night, even though we were both so tired and had come so far," Alice recalls. "So much had happened in both of our lives. We must have hugged for hours."

Early the following January, on the way back to Michigan, Alice's sister was killed in a traffic accident. Already back in Colorado, Alice gathered funds and flew to Michigan, where her sister had wanted to be buried with her husband.

Throughout the funeral, Alice again remembered the three Indian men who had helped her. Without them, she likely would not have survived the storm and would certainly not have gotten to reconcile with her sister.

"I asked myself continually why they had come to help me," Alice says. "Over and over, I wondered about them. The whites had been so awful to them, but they had saved my life. I know the history about the battle now, but that seems so incredible to me. It was real, though. That night was so very real. I shall never forget it."

Index

EARL MURRAY, among the most acclaimed of modern-day novelists of the Western frontier, is a former botanist and rangeland conservationist with a lifelong interest in Indian lore. Among his Forge books are *Spirit of the Moon*, *The Flaming Sky*, *Song of Wovoka*, and *Thunder in the Dawn*. He lives in Fort Collins, Colorado.